Masculinities at the Margins

Across a rich terrain of empirical and theoretical trajectories, the concept of military masculinity (now understood in its plural as military masculinities) has been a significant conceptual tool in both feminist international relations (IR) and in critical men and masculinities studies scholarship. The concept has helped us to unpack the relationships between gender, war, and militarism, including how military standards function in the production of wider normative, hegemonic manliness. As such, military masculinities has been a rewarding tool for many scholars who take a critical approach to the study of war and the military.

This edited volume advances an emerging curiosity within accounts of military masculinities. This curiosity concerns the silences within, and disruptions to, our well-established and perhaps-too-comfortable understandings of, and empirical focal points for, military masculinities, gender, and war. The contributors to this volume trouble the ease with which we might be tempted to synonymize militaries, war, and a neat, 'hegemonic' masculinity. Taking the disruptions, the asides, and the silences seriously challenges the common wisdoms of military masculinities, gender, and war in productive and necessary ways. Doing so necessitates a reorientation of where, to whom, and for what we look to understand the operation of gendered military power.

The chapters were originally published in a special issue of *Critical Military Studies*.

Amanda Chisholm is Senior Lecturer in Security Studies at Kings College London, London, UK and a feminist scholar who contributes to the growing field of critical gender studies on private military and security companies (PMSCs). Her research is rooted at the crossroads of feminist global political economy (GPE) and feminist critical security studies, and she is currently the Primary Investigator on an Economic and Social Council Research grant, 'From Military to Market'. Amanda's research appears in *Security Dialogue, Globalizations, Critical Military Studies, International Political Sociology* and *International Journal of Feminist Politics*.

Joanna Tidy is Lecturer in Politics in the Department of Politics at the University of Sheffield, UK. Across her work she has been concerned with the gendered politics of knowledge underpinning the possibility, conduct, and contestation of war. Her latest work has been published in journals including *International Political Sociology, Review of International Studies, Critical Military Studies,* and the *International Feminist Journal of Politics*. She is currently researching and writing a book on gender and war beyond combat. https://www.sheffield.ac.uk/politics/people/academic/joanna-tidy/profile.

Masculinities at the Margins

Beyond the Hegemonic in the Study
of Militaries, Masculinities and War

Edited by
Amanda Chisholm and Joanna Tidy

LONDON AND NEW YORK

First published 2019
by Routledge
2 Park Square, Milton Park, Abingdon, Oxon, OX14 4RN, UK

and by Routledge
711 Third Avenue, New York, NY 10017, USA

Routledge is an imprint of the Taylor & Francis Group, an informa business

© 2019 Taylor & Francis

British Library Cataloguing-in-Publication Data
A catalogue record for this book is available from the British Library

ISBN13: 978-1-138-54196-2

Typeset in Minion Pro
by codeMantra

Publisher's Note
The publisher accepts responsibility for any inconsistencies that may have arisen during the conversion of this book from journal articles to book chapters, namely the possible inclusion of journal terminology.

Disclaimer
Every effort has been made to contact copyright holders for their permission to reprint material in this book. The publishers would be grateful to hear from any copyright holder who is not here acknowledged and will undertake to rectify any errors or omissions in future editions of this book.

Contents

Citation Information

The chapters in this book were originally published in *Critical Military Studies*, volume 3, issue 2 (August 2017). When citing this material, please use the original page numbering for each article, as follows:

Chapter 1
Beyond the hegemonic in the study of militaries, masculinities, and war
Amanda Chisholm and Joanna Tidy
Critical Military Studies, volume 3, issue 2 (August 2017) pp. 99–102

Chapter 2
Re-thinking hegemonic masculinities in conflict-affected contexts
Henri Myrttinen, Lana Khattab and Jana Naujoks
Critical Military Studies, volume 3, issue 2 (August 2017) pp. 103–119

Chapter 3
Clients, contractors, and the everyday masculinities in global private security
Amanda Chisholm
Critical Military Studies, volume 3, issue 2 (August 2017) pp. 120–141

Chapter 4
Combat as a moving target: masculinities, the heroic soldier myth, and normative martial violence
Katharine M. Millar and Joanna Tidy
Critical Military Studies, volume 3, issue 2 (August 2017) pp. 142–160

Chapter 5
Unmaking militarized masculinity: veterans and the project of military-to-civilian transition
Sarah Bulmer and Maya Eichler
Critical Military Studies, volume 3, issue 2 (August 2017) pp. 161–181

Chapter 6
Problematizing military masculinity, intersectionality and male vulnerability in feminist critical military studies
Marsha Henry
Critical Military Studies, volume 3, issue 2 (August 2017) pp. 182–199

Chapter 7

What's the problem with the concept of military masculinities?
Marysia Zalewski
Critical Military Studies, volume 3, issue 2 (August 2017) pp. 200–205

Chapter 8

Living archives and Cyprus: militarized masculinities and decolonial emerging world horizons
Anna M. Agathangelou
Critical Military Studies, volume 3, issue 2 (August 2017) pp. 206–211

For any permission-related enquiries please visit:
http://www.tandfonline.com/page/help/permissions

Notes on Contributors

Anna M. Agathangelou is Associate Professor in the Department of Politics at York University, Toronto, Canada.

Sarah Bulmer is Senior Lecturer in Critical Military Studies and International Relations in the Department of Politics at the University of Exeter, Penryn, UK.

Amanda Chisholm is Senior Lecturer in Security Studies at Kings College London, London, UK.

Maya Eichler is Canada Research Chair in Social Innovation and Community Engagement and Assistant Professor in Political and Canadian Studies and Women's Studies at Mount Saint Vincent University, Halifax, Canada.

Marsha Henry is Associate Professor and Deputy Director of the Centre for Women, Peace and Security at the London School of Economics and Political Science, Gender Institute, UK.

Lana Khattab is a Specialist for the Durable Solutions Platform at the Danish Refugee Council, Jordan.

Katharine M. Millar is Assistant Professor of International Relations in the Department of International Relations at the London School of Economics, UK.

Henri Myrttinen is Head of Gender and Peacebuilding at International Alert, London, UK.

Jana Naujoks is a Consultant to International Alert's Myanmar team, advising on Gender and Research, at International Alert, London, UK.

Joanna Tidy is Lecturer in Politics in the Department of Politics at the University of Sheffield, UK.

Marysia Zalewski is Professor of International Relations and Director of People & Environment in the School of Law & Politics at Cardiff University, UK.

Preface

Amanda Chisholm and Joanna Tidy

This collection represents a moment in an unfolding conversation concerning the development and deployment of the concept of military/ised masculinities. The ideas and concerns explored here continue to animate the work not just, of course, of those contributors whose pieces are collected here but also a wide group of scholars. We, in that broadest sense, continue to reflect on the provocations, cautions, new directions and possibilities that are outlined in this collection and beyond.

In a recent rejoinder in *Critical Military Studies*,[1] Marsha Henry further considers what she terms the 'repoliticisation' of intersectionality within research on militarised masculinities and highlights how, both in contributions to this special issue and beyond,[2] authors have successfully politicised "which and when differences matter; why inequalities persist; and where military men and women are not equally positioned or privileged". Henry's timely warning against a re-politicised use of intersectionality, one which erases the historical roots of the term when it only considers diversity and difference and does not examine multiple oppressions, was a critique and challenge addressed by, for example, Megan Daigle and Henri Myrttinen in their research examining vulnerabilities of persons of diverse sexual orientation and gender identity in conflict-affected societies.[3] Exploring avenues for theorising war and masculinity beyond its locus in 'combat' and 'combatant bodies', a recent article in *International Political Sociology* by Joanna Tidy theorises fatherhood masculinities in relation to war, moving analyses of 'men in war' beyond a focus on soldiers and perpetrators and charting the "intersecting terms of privilege and subordination" through which differently racialised subjects are granted or denied particular forms of intelligible political subjectivity.[4] In a blog piece at www.gender andwar.com, David Duriesmith takes Marysia Zalewski's suggestion, in this special issue, that military masculinities has become "overly familiar and comfortable". From this starting point Duriesmith considers the concern that "'militarised masculinities' has centred European military institutions as the natural and inevitable holders of collective violence".[5]

Drawing attention to these few very recent, and in no way exhaustive, examples, we have hoped to show how, rather than the culmination of a conversation, the special issue reproduced in this volume forms part of a very active ongoing collaboration and exchange. We would like to once again thank the contributors and the wider community of colleagues whose work continues to keep us excited, challenged and uneasy!

Notes

1. Marsha, G. H. (2018) 'Why critical military studies needs to smash imperial white supremacist capitalist heteropatriarchy: a rejoinder', *Critical Military Studies*, doi: 10.1080/23337486.2018.1429049.
2. Ingelaere, B., & Wilén, N. (2017) 'The civilised Self and the barbaric Other: Ex-rebels making sense of sexual violence in the DR Congo', *Journal of Contemporary African Studies*, 35(2),

221–239; Myrttinen, H. (2018) 'Men, masculinities and genocide' in *A gendered lens for genocide prevention* (pp. 27–47) Palgrave Macmillan, London; Partis-Jennings, H. (2017) 'Military masculinity and the act of killing in Hamlet and Afghanistan', *Men and Masculinities*, doi: 10.1177/1097184X17718585; Richter-Montpetit, M. (2016) 'Militarized masculinities, women torturers, and the limits of gender analysis at Abu Ghraib' in *Researching war: Feminist methods, ethics and politics* (pp. 92–116) Routledge, London; Barkawi, T. (2017) *Soldiers of empire.* Cambridge University Press, Cambridge; Burnett, S., & Milani, T. M. (2017) 'Fatal masculinities: A queer look at green violence', *ACME: An International Journal for Critical Geographies,* 16(3), 548–575.

3. Daigle, M., & Myrttinen, H. (2018) 'Bringing diverse sexual orientation and gender identity (SOGI) into peacebuilding policy and practice', *Gender & Development*, 26(1), 103–120.
4. Tidy, J. (2018) 'Fatherhood, gender and interventions in the geopolitical: Analysing paternal peace, masculinities and war', *International Political Sociology*, 12(1): 2–18.
5. Duriesmith, D. (2017) 'De-centring 'militarisation' in the study of collective masculine violence', available at: http://www.genderandwar.com/2017/12/18/de-centring-militarisation-in-the-study-of-collective-masculine-violence/.

Beyond the hegemonic in the study of militaries, masculinities, and war

Amanda Chisholm ⓘ and Joanna Tidy

Across a rich terrain of empirical and theoretical trajectories, the concept of military masculinity (now understood in its plural as military masculinities) has been a significant conceptual tool in both feminist international relations (IR) and in critical men and masculinities studies scholarship. The concept has helped us to unpack the relationships between gender, war, and militarism (Enloe 1993; 2000), including how military standards function in the production of wider normative, hegemonic (Connell 1995; Connell and Messerschmidt 2005; Agathangelou and Ling 2009) manliness. As such, military masculinities has been a rewarding tool for many scholars who take a critical approach to the study of war and the military, enabling us to approach 'military power as a question rather than taking it for granted' (Basham, Belkin, and Gifkins 2015, 1) and deconstruct areas of 'common sense' (Enloe 2004, 1–3) through which gendered military power is reproduced.

This special issue advances what we identify as an emerging curiosity within accounts of military masculinities. This curiosity concerns the silences within and disruptions to our well-established and perhaps too comfortable understandings of and empirical focal points for military masculinities, gender, and war. The special issue is situated within emerging critiques of military masculinities. Scholars such as Stachowitsch (2015), Richter-Montpetit (2007), Howell (2007), and Belkin (2012) all expand where we locate gendered militarist logics of war and its various contestations. In common with these scholars, the contributors to this special issue trouble the ease with which we might be tempted to synonymize militaries, war, and a neat, 'hegemonic' masculinity. Taking the disruptions, the asides, and the silences seriously, we claim, challenges the common wisdoms of military masculinities, gender, and war in productive and necessary ways.

Doing so, we argue, necessitates a re-orientation of where, to whom, and for what we look to understand the operation of gendered military power. It involves paying attention to the margins and the marginal, variously characterized, of masculinities and war. It prompts us to consider how concepts originating from marginal knowledges can be applied to the study of military masculinities, and our responsibilities to the political projects in which they are grounded. It challenges us to ask how gendered military power is (re)produced within our own conceptualizations. It also necessitates looking beyond soldiers to other people, other bodies, and other subjectivities of war –

to non-combatants, to veterans, and to the researcher – to understand military masculinities and war. This special issue gathers scholars from various backgrounds who each begin with one or more of these provocations. Individually and collectively they challenge us to reorient and reconceptualize military masculinities, and war, beyond the hegemonic.

In their piece 'Re-thinking Hegemonic Masculinities in Conflict-Affected Contexts', Henri Myrttinen, Lana Khattab, and Jana Naujoks offer rich empirical insights that push the account of masculinities in conflict-affected and peacebuilding contexts beyond the narrow focus on 'men and their violences' and simplified accounts of hegemonic and hyper masculinities. They consider the absence of non-combatants, displaced persons, and non-heterosexual masculinities, and call for re-examination and re-articulation of the idea of 'hegemonic masculinity', and a widening of the scope of study. Amanda Chisholm, in her 'Clients, Contractors, and the Everyday Masculinities in Global Private Security', also offers both an empirical and a methodological intervention, with an explicit focus on the gendered and racialized relations between the scholar who researches security and her research community. Employing an autoethnographic examination of her research of private security contractors in Kabul, Afghanistan, and placing herself as the main analytical focus, Chisholm shows us how the knowledge we produce about militarism, violence, and gender cannot be separated from our own embodiments and gender biases that will always frame our research questions and mediate how we navigate and write about the field. Both Myrttinen, Khattab, and Naujoks and Chisholm re-orientate our focal points for the embodiment and production of military masculinities.

In their contribution 'Combat as a Moving Target: Masculinities, the Heroic Soldier Myth and Normative Martial Violence', Katharine M. Millar and Joanna Tidy interrogate the gendered politics of conceptualizing 'combat' within masculinities theorizing. They trace how combat has been mobilized as a common-sense empirical category within critical feminist and gender analyses, importing its normative investments. Millar and Tidy argue that this has obscured the political work that masculinities do to constitute 'combat', as an imagination of normative violence, with this imagination sustaining 'military authority and the broader social acceptance of war'. Sarah Bulmer and Maya Eichler's 'Unmaking Militarized Masculinity: Veterans and the Project of Military-to-Civilian Transition' argues for a focus on the unmaking rather than the making of militarized masculinity. They explore the experiences of veterans transitioning to civilian life, arguing that 'attempts to unmake militarized masculinity in the figure of the veteran challenge' key aspects of feminist analyses of war and militarization. 'Embodied veteran identities refuse a totalizing conception of what militarized masculinity might be' as well as demonstrating 'the limits of efforts to exceptionalize the military'.

Both Millar and Tidy's and Bulmer and Eichler's work speaks to a need to pluralize military and militarized experiences and to be analytically careful with the concepts we use as critical scholars. Marsha Henry shares this impulse in her 'Problematizing Military Masculinity, Intersectionality and Male Vulnerability in Feminist Critical Military Studies'. Her article traces the use of intersectionality in work on the multiplicity, hierarchies within, and vulnerabilities of military masculinities. She raises the importance of connecting these analyses to the '"originary" black feminist project' from which intersectionality has been drawn, and ponders cautionary answers to the question of our responsibilities in using concepts such as intersectionality, black and double consciousness, standpoint, and situated knowledges. Consequently, Henry reminds us of the politics of how we understand and apply the very concepts we use to understand militarism, gender, and war.

In her Encounters contribution, Marysia Zalewski asks 'What's the Problem with the Concept of Military Masculinities?' Sharing a scepticism concerning current iterations of the concept within feminist scholarship with the contributors above, Zalewski takes as her point of departure the 'idea that the concept of military masculinities has become overly familiar and "comfortable", at least within feminist scholarship, and that this "cosiness" is problematic'. Catherine Baker, reflecting upon Holly Furneaux's recent book *Military Men of Feeling* (2016) in her Encounters contribution, demonstrates how archetypes of hegemonic masculinities – embodied in the stiff upper lip, emotionally constrained, physically fit combat soldier, were also challenged in alternative histories of British military operations. She draws our attention to the important work on militarism, gender, and war being produced outside feminist IR spaces. Finally, in her Encounters piece, Anna Agathangelou offers a de-colonial feminist critique of military masculinities. Taking the concept outside a western academy and drawing upon 'living' archival histories of her mother's stories of war and violence in Cyprus, Agathangelou gives an important alternative voice to our understanding of military masculinities – and challenges our own western-centric ideas concerning the universality of militarism, gender, and war.

The contributors to this special issue, in different ways, reconsider, push beyond, or complicate the well-worn associations that link hegemonic masculinity, militaries, and war. Each research article and Encounters piece speaks to unease with existing theoretical configurations of the masculinities–militaries–war nexus. They all illuminate the way in which 'military masculinities' has in some important regards become a form of comfortable story, the ending to which we seem to already know. Yet, as they reveal the silences, disruptions, and erasures that structure the comfortable story of military masculinities, our contributors also make this conceptual and empirical terrain newly strange (see Eriksson and Stern 2016, 117). Another way to think about it is that each of our contributors applies a feminist curiosity (Enloe 2004, 2015) back onto the concept of military masculinities, converting the comfortable givens of the well-worn masculinities story into questions. In doing so they open up new avenues and possible directions for future scholarship. As such, this special issue comes – to butcher Shakespeare – not to bury military masculinities (although we have all probably felt like doing so at one point or another!). Neither does it unquestioningly come to praise the concept by mobilizing it as a common-sense critical scholarly panacea. Rather, we aim to offer some possible ways in which to keep the concept curious, sceptical, and uncomfortable.

Acknowledgements

We thank our contributing authors for giving us so much to think about in each of their pieces. We also thank them for their patience with the editorial process. We thank Victoria Basham and the whole *Critical Military Studies* team for building the intellectual space that this journal represents and for facilitating the publication of this special issue. We thank the reviewers who contributed their time and intellectual labour. And we thank all participants in the workshop *Masculinities at the Margins: War beyond Hypermasculinity* (Newcastle University, 22–24 April 2015) where the seeds of this issue's interventions were first sown.

Disclosure statement

No potential conflict of interest was reported by the authors.

ORCID

Amanda Chisholm ⓘ http://orcid.org/0000-0001-9008-2529

References

Agathangelou, A.M., and L.H.M. Ling. 2009. *Transforming world politics: From empire to multiple worlds*. Abington: Routledge.

Basham, V.M., A. Belkin, and J. Gifkins. 2015. What is critical military studies? *Critical Military Studies* 1, no. 1: 1–3. doi:10.1080/23337486.2015.1006879

Belkin, A. 2012. *Bring me men: Military masculinity and the benign façade of American empire 1898-2001*. New York: Columbia University Press.

Connell, R.W. 1995. *Masculinities*. Cambridge: Polity Press.

Connell, R.W., and J.W. Messerschmidt. 2005. Hegemonic masculinity rethinking the concept. *Gender & Society* 19, no. 6: 829–59. doi:10.1177/0891243205278639

Enloe, C. 1993. *The morning after: Sexual politics at the end of the Cold War*. Berkeley: University of California Press.

Enloe, C. 2000. *Maneuvers: The international politics of militarizing women's lives*. Los Angeles: University of California Press.

Enloe, C. 2004. *The curious feminist: Searching for women in a new age of empire*. Los Angeles: University of California Press.

Enloe, C. 2015. The recruiter and the sceptic: A critical feminist approach to military studies. *Critical Military Studies* 1, no. 1: 3–10. doi:10.1080/23337486.2014.961746

Eriksson, B., and M. Stern. 2016. Researching wartime rape in the Democratic Republic of Congo: A methodology of unease. In *Researching war: Feminist methods, ethics and politics*, ed. A.T. Wibben. London & New York: Routledge.

Furneaux, H. 2016. *Military men of feeling*. Oxon: Oxford University Press.

Howell, A. 2007. Victims or madmen? The diagnosis competition over "terrorist" Detainees at guantanamo bay. *International Political Sociology* 1, no. 1: 29–47. doi:10.1111/j.1749-5687.2007.00003.x

Richter-Montpetit, M. 2007. Empire, desire and violence: A queer transnational feminist reading of the prisoner 'abuse' in abu ghraib and the question of gender equality. *International Feminist Journal of Politics* 9, no. 1: 38–59. doi:10.1080/14616740601066366

Stachowitsch, S. 2015. The reconstruction of masculinities in global politics: Gendering strategies in the field of private security. *Men and Masculinities* 18, no. 3: 363–86. doi:10.1177/1097184X14551205

Re-thinking hegemonic masculinities in conflict-affected contexts

Henri Myrttinen, Lana Khattab and Jana Naujoks

ABSTRACT

Masculinities in conflict-affected and peacebuilding contexts have generally speaking been under-researched. Much of the existing research focuses relatively narrowly on men and their 'violences', especially that of combatants. Conceptually, much of the policy debate has revolved around either men's 'innate' propensity to violence or relatively simplistic uses of frameworks such as hegemonic, military/militarized, or 'hyper'-masculinities. These discourses have often been reinforced and reproduced without relating them to their respective local historical, political, and socio-economic contexts. In academic circles, the discussion is more advanced and progressive, but this has yet to filter through to on-the-ground work.

Considering the overwhelming role men play in producing and reproducing conflict-related and other forms of violence, a better understanding of the links between masculinities and violence – as well as non-violence – should be central to examining gender, conflict, and peace. Nonetheless, currently a large part of masculinities are side-lined in research, such as those of non-combatants or displaced persons, the associated challenges of 'thwarted masculinities', or the positive agency of peacebuilders. Non-heterosexual masculinities also are largely invisible. Based on recent multi-country field research, we aim to highlight some of the under-researched issues revolving around conflict-affected masculinities while also discussing some conceptual challenges arising as a result. Our two key arguments are that the notion of 'hegemonic masculinities' in conflict-affected situations needs to be re-examined and re-articulated in more nuanced ways, and that the scope of studying masculinities in these situations needs to be broadened to go beyond merely examining the violences of men.

1. Introduction

While the roles and dimensions of masculinities in conflict and war are increasingly being acknowledged among academic circles, and slowly also among 'practitioners', for lack of a better term, the research has tended to be focused on certain groups and to employ a relatively narrow scope. Much of the research and studies on men and masculinities in conflict have focused on highlighting the various 'violences' associated with them, often focusing exclusively on actors such as intervening soldiers, military

5

peacekeepers, warlords, combatants, and ex-combatants; and the various forms of domestic, sexual, and gender-based violence (SGBV) within and beyond households frequently framed with a focus on men as perpetrators. This focus on the 'violences of men' (Hearn 1998) was a key concern of many of the early works of critical masculinity studies (Connell 1987, 1995; Kimmel 1987; and Messner 1990), while peace and conflict studies have sometimes taken a somewhat biologically deterministic approach to men and violence (e.g. Johan Galtung as critiqued by Confortini 2006; or Ignatieff 1998). The fields of critical military/security studies (e.g. Barrett 1996; Chisholm 2014; Haaland 2012; Higate 2003) along with in-depth ethnographic studies of combatant and formerly combatant men (e.g. Eriksson Baaz and Stern 2009; Hoffman 2011; Vigh 2006) have grown vastly over the past decades. Arguably, critical approaches to masculinities in the Non-Governmental Organisation (NGO) sector, including our own work and to a degree that of others (Myrttinen, Naujoks, and El-Bushra 2014; Wright 2014), has also tended to focus more on the violences of men and men who have committed violence than non-violence.

This focus is on the one hand understandable: conflict-affected situations are defined precisely by these violences, and men and boys are by and large the main perpetrators of these violences globally. On the other hand, the focus leaves out the masculinities which are not violent and the men and boys embodying these masculinities. This body of research has been absolutely critical to opening up debates on masculinities in conflict-affected situations as well as deepening our understanding of the links between violence and gendered norms, roles, and expectations. However, this focus has meant that men as peacebuilders and non-violent men, who by and large are the majority of men even in conflict-affected situations, have seldom been researched or theorized, especially from a critical gender perspective. The exception would be the examination of individual men, such as idolized icons like Mahatma Gandhi, Martin Luther King Jr., or Nelson Mandela (e.g. Reychler and Stellamans 2003; Steger 2001), or those who have made an individual effort of 'betterment' (often as part of NGO and/or faith-based interventions) and change to become better fathers, less violent husbands, or the like (for a constructive critique of these interventions, see for example Dworkin et al. 2012; Gibbs et al. 2015; Myrttinen 2015).

As the peacebuilding policy sphere and those involved in the practical implementation of these policies are increasingly looking to engage with 'men and boys as actors of positive change', the need to better understand the violences and non-violences of men becomes more acute. Conceptually, however, much of the debate in NGOs', national governments', and international agencies' circles on peacebuilding seems at times trapped in discourses that either revolve around essentialist arguments highlighting men's 'innate' propensity to violence, or focus on simplistic uses of frameworks such as hegemonic, military/militarized, or 'hyper'-masculinities.[1] Problematically, these discourses have also often been reinforced and reproduced without relating them to their respective historical, political, and socio-economic contexts – an issue which we, as part of our daily work in an international peacebuilding organization, encounter repeatedly in our interactions with various national and international actors. This is the case both for the international policy frameworks on gender, peace, and security, as discussed below, and for the policy debates which frame and are framed by them. Local- and national-level actors often feel compelled to use the language as well as the theoretical frameworks of the Global North in order to be heard, forcing them to drop local complexity and nuance. At the same time, international actors often pay lip service to an openness towards ambiguity, but in practice demand simple, quick answers to complex, messy, long-term issues.

In a sense, the use of 'hegemonic masculinities' as an entry point to critically examine and challenge men's violences and militarization has been a victim of its own success – at least in terms of its use in women, peace, and security (WPS)-related policy spheres. Military masculinities have rightly been critiqued for the reproduction of violence, oppression of the weak, misogyny, homophobia, and racism (e.g. Whitworth 2004), and the military has been critiqued as a site of production of hegemonic masculinity (e.g. Kronsell 2005). While the academics formulating such critiques most likely did not intend it so, these critiques have in the policy and 'practitioner' field often been reduced to simplistic approaches, equating violence and hegemonic masculinity, military/militarized masculinities, and violent, homophobic, and misogynistic behaviour; and hegemonic masculinity with military/militarized masculinities, thus working on the premise that violent, military masculinities are hegemonic, especially in conflict-affected societies.[2]

In terms of the broader WPS policy architecture, men and boys, and their masculinities, have mostly been invisible. When they are mentioned, it is mostly implicitly as perpetrators of violence (often utilizing the language of violent/hegemonic/militarized masculinities), but occasionally also as potential partners for positive change and as potential victims, in particular of conflict-related sexual violence. As Kirby and Shepherd (2016, 252) note:

> WPS refers not to women alone in the context of peace and security, but to gender, peace and security. Men feature in WPS frequently as the perpetrators of violence or as potential allies in seeking gender equality; but also, increasingly, as a constituency that is itself at risk in certain situations.

The degree to which men, boys, and masculinities are invisible or highlighted as violent/militarized was evident also in the 'Global Study' on Women, Peace and Security (UN Women 2015). In 2014–2015, United Nations (UN) Women co-ordinated a global review process of 15 years of implementing UN Security Council Resolution 1325 as part of a UN-mandated High Level Review process. In the 418 pages of the Global Study, 'boys' are mentioned five times in relation to their educational performance compared to girls; 'men and boys' are mentioned once as potential combatants and once as receiving preferential treatment to 'women and girls' when it comes to nutrition; the possibilities of changing of male behaviour are mentioned five times; and masculinities are mentioned twice in the context of 'violent masculinities' and twice as 'militarized masculinities'. Men and boys come up 13 times as part of the phrase 'men, women, boys and girls'. LGBT (lesbian, gay, bisexual, trans – the 'I' for intersex is not used in the document) persons are mentioned twice. These figures, as low as they are, are however somewhat inflated by the fact that a number of these mentions are made twice, when the phrase in question is used in the main text and the summarizing bullet points at the end of a section.

We argue that this glossing over of men, boys, and masculinities in conflict-affected situations, the imprecise use of theories of hegemonic masculinities, and the focus mainly on men's violences are a missed opportunity. Men and masculinities are a central factor in re-producing but also potentially ending patterns of violent conflict. Therefore, going beyond the dominant and traditionally researched roles and actors of masculinity in conflict and peacebuilding contexts allows us to identify and examine various other forms of masculinities that are frequently overlooked in order to strengthen the current analytical frameworks. As much as the hegemonic masculinities approach has helped us in thinking critically about conflict-affected masculinities, a broader, more contextualized approach is necessary. It is also necessary in our minds to take a more relational approach – examining how men and women together co-produce masculinities, and how these are produced in relation to other forms of being a man and in relation to femininities (El-Bushra 2012; Myrttinen, Naujoks, and El-Bushra 2014). Embracing such an approach will enable us to have a more holistic picture of gender dynamics in given contexts, and allow for a more nuanced analysis and more targeted peacebuilding initiatives.

Among other sources, this paper will primarily draw on findings from recent multi-country field research we conducted in Lebanon, Burundi, Nepal, Colombia, and Uganda.[3] The research was part of different peacebuilding projects of International Alert and consisted mainly of focus group discussions, individual interviews (all with men and women of different ages, as well as, in cases where it was possible, persons self-identifying outside of binary gender identities) and the analysis of secondary data. Most of the interviewees were current or returned refugees and displaced persons, former combatants, active members of security-sector institutions, members of the state administration, NGO activists, and academics.

Following a brief critique of the usefulness of 'hegemonic masculinities' in conflict-affected situations, we will focus here on three mostly understudied aspects of conflict-affected masculinities: 'thwarted' masculinities, male vulnerabilities, and men not conforming to heterosexual norms/gender binaries.

2. The uses and limitations of hegemonic masculinities

The work of Connell (1987, 1995) has provided a valuable theoretical framework for conceptualizing masculinities which takes into account the implications of power relations and processes of socialization. As a starting point to the framework, Connell states the 'structural fact' of global dominance of men over women. She argues that this power hierarchy provides the main basis for relationships among men, favouring a 'hegemonic' form of masculinity. In other words, 'hegemonic masculinity' is always constructed in relation to subordinated masculinities and women. Connell's understanding of 'hegemony' is based on a Gramscian definition and is thus understood as a structural relation: 'It is the successful claim to authority, more than direct violence that is the mark of hegemony' (Connell 1995, 77).

Although Connell's framework does not simply oppose 'masculinity' to 'femininity', it acknowledges the power hierarchies and argues for taking a historical and contextual perspective, yet a number of critiques highlight the concept's shortcomings. Martin (1998) highlights the ambiguity and confusion in the usage of the term 'hegemonic masculinity'. While it is supposed to designate whatever masculinity is dominant at a given time, it is often used to simplistically indicate negative 'types' of violent and/or militarized masculinities, which undermines the concept's utility (Martin 1998).

Furthermore, Connell does not always herself use hegemony in its Gramscian sense, but rather there is widespread slippage between hegemonic in this sense, hegemonic as denoting 'the most powerful', or hegemonic as referring to 'the most widespread' in masculinity studies in general and (though to a lesser degree) in Connell's work (Beasley 2008).

The concept of hegemonic masculinities has been useful in opening up debates on male gender norms. However, as the critique of the past 15 years has shown, it can also be a victim of its own success. It is at times used as a catchy stock phrase that has lost its analytical value and one that is often used in an ahistoric, West-centric, and conceptually overly rigid manner. Using the concept tends to evoke in the listener or reader an immediate sense of seemingly knowing what or who is meant, yet the process of how hegemonic masculinities play out in men's and women's lives differs in every context, changing through time and space, but also depending on the frame of analysis. Thus, what counts as hegemonic is not fixed but is constantly subject to contestation and alteration (Wetherell and Edley 1999). The critiques point towards the danger of an oversimplification of the concept, by using it in a broad sense without more contextually specific analysis. In spite of the critique of Connell's framing of masculinities, no other similarly influential conceptual framework has emerged to replace it, and the study of seemingly 'hegemonic' masculinities tends to overshadow the studying of other forms of masculinities in conflict and peacebuilding contexts.

The conflation of hegemony, violence, the military (or other militarized institutions such as militias or guerrillas), and masculinity, while powerful as a critique, can be problematic from an analytical point of view. We identify at least four fundamental problems with it. First, hegemony does not necessarily require violence, at least not if one uses the term in its Gramscian sense, unless there is widespread societal buy-in for this violence, including from those in subordinate positions. This may exist for certain forms of violence in the private sphere (e.g. societal acceptance of corporal punishment of children or of a degree of domestic violence), but usually not for violence in the public sphere, unless this is accepted as being for the common good and regulated by norms and institutions (e.g. entrusted to and carried out by a group seen as having the legitimacy to protect the community, such as the armed forces). Second, the use of physical violence is often not viewed societally as a hallmark of respectable or hegemonic masculinity. In fact, the opposite may be the case, with subordinate men (be it hired thugs, low-ranking soldiers, and police officers or private security guards) carrying out physical violence on behalf of socio-economically more powerful men (Chisholm 2014; De Silva 2005; Higate 2012; Khattab and Myrttinen forthcoming; Myrttinen 2010). Third, being a member of the military or a military-like institution is not necessarily the most accepted or most respected, let alone the most hegemonic, way of being a man, even in conflict-affected situations. The military or insurgents may be seen by affected communities as unwanted outsiders, while unarmed, civilian community leaders are treated with far more respect (Udasmoro, Myrttinen, and Kunz forthcoming). The ways of being a man in the military, especially a lower ranking soldier, or an insurgent, may be closer to Connell's subordinate and protest masculinities rather than hegemonic masculinity. Lastly, in spite of clear links between male-dominated military/militarized institutions, the use of violence which is central to their raison d'être, and the kinds of masculinities promoted and constructed within them, the connection between military masculinities and violence is often complex, and at times contradictory, rather than a straightforward endorsement of violent masculine behaviour (see for example Barrett 1996; Belkin 2012; Duncanson 2013; Haaland 2012; Higate 2003; Myrttinen 2003; Myrttinen, Naujoks, and El-Bushra 2014; Tidy 2015; Titunik 2008; Wright 2014b).

Men in our research often faced contradictory expectations that do not fit easily with a one-dimensional notion of violent masculinities being hegemonic in conflict-affected situations. Men and women are confronted by the need to take up new roles in conflict-affected situations while the underlying gender norms may remain the same. The ensuing expectations can be contradictory, including in relation to the use of violence. In the Syrian case, for example, protecting, providing, and caring for one's community and family was an impetus for some men to take up arms and for others to flee (Khattab and Myrttinen forthcoming). In the following sections we explore in more detail three aspects which have often fallen outside of the debates on conflict-affected men and masculinities: 'thwarted' masculinities, male vulnerabilities, and the situation of non-heterosexual men.

2.1. 'Thwarted' masculinities

One of the more researched non-dominant forms of conflict-affected masculinities is that of 'thwarted' masculinities (for example Dolan 2002, 2009; Moore 1994; Kabachnik et al. 2013; Kesmaecker-Wissing and Pagot 2015; Vigh 2006). This refers to the masculinities of men who are bound by expectations of living up to dominant notions of masculinity in the face of realities which make it practically impossible to achieve these, leading to frustration and at times various forms of violence, against both others and oneself.

Conflict and displacement tend to involve a shift in traditional gender roles which often do not fit well with traditional gender norms and expectations, with women taking up traditionally masculine-coded roles and men struggling to live up to notions of being decision-makers, protectors, and breadwinners. Our research in northern Uganda (El-Bushra, Naujoks, and Myrttinen 2014) examined gender roles in a context marked by decades of conflict and displacement. This had resulted in large numbers of forced migrants, with around two million internally displaced people (IDPs) within northern Uganda at the turn of the millennium and persistently significant numbers displaced across state borders, mainly from Democratic Republic of Congo (DR Congo) and Burundi. IDPs in the Acholi sub-region of northern Uganda had often spent years in camps, exposed to high levels of insecurity, economic hardship, violence, and torture, including SGBV against women and men, and consequent difficulties in fulfilling expected gender roles, and were now re-building their lives in their home villages (El-Bushra, Naujoks, and Myrttinen 2014).

A closer analysis of the context of displacement and life in camps (and to a degree also upon returning to villages) revealed that men are unable to fulfil their primary role as provider for their family: men lost the power derived from their role as managers of the two major resources – cattle and arable land – while new livelihoods offered women and youth opportunities for economic independence (Dolan 2002, 2009). The 'ideal man' is expected to protect his family and provide for the material needs of women and children, but the reality of life in the displaced camps prevented them from doing so. The limited livelihood opportunities caused by the loss of Acholi cattle and the dependence on irregular food aid made it very difficult for men to live up to expectations of 'ideal' masculinity. While the ideal man is characterized by being married and begetting children, many men were unable to put together the required bride-wealth in cattle or in cash. This meant that they could not be accorded the status of 'adult' (El-Bushra and Sahl 2005). 'Ordinary' men were unable to provide protection for their families from attacks by the Lord's Resistance Army (LRA) and the Uganda People's Defence Force (UPDF). Skill in the use of dialogue rather than aggression as a means of solving problems – another marker of 'ideal' masculinity – became impossible, given the intractable nature of many problems facing people. Thus, Acholi men were 'thwarted' at every turn which, coupled with the general exposure to violence and the resulting trauma, led to intense frustration and destructive behaviour directed at those around them and at themselves, in the form of domestic violence, criminal violence, alcoholism, and suicide (Dolan 2009).

Similar gaps between expectations of masculinity compared to the physical, political, economic, and social impossibilities of achieving them in conflict-affected situations, and the ensuing frustrations, are also documented for example in Burundi (Turner 1999), DR Congo (Kesmaecker-Wissing and Pagot 2015), and Georgia (Kabachnik et al. 2013), and also in our research on Syrian refugees in neighbouring countries (Khattab and Myrttinen forthcoming). As Dolan (2002, 64) has noted, in the 'context of on-going war, heavy militarisation and internal displacement it is very difficult, if not impossible for the vast majority of men to fulfil the expectations contained in the model of masculinity' prevalent as the idealized form in society. Nonetheless, Dolan (2001, 11) argues that

> the normative model of masculinity [...] exercises considerable power over men, precisely because they are unable to behave according to it, but cannot afford not to try to live up to it. The relationship between the social and political acceptance which comes from being seen to conform to the norm, and access to a variety of resources, is a critical one in a conflict situation.

The frustration and violence caused by the inability to live up to expected norms have at times been inadvertently exacerbated by outside actors, such as NGOs and national agencies: seemingly gender-sensitive programming for refugees and IDPs has at times translated into focusing support on women, in line with widespread assumptions that women are more likely than men to use resources for the benefit of the family rather than for themselves. However, this rationale is rarely explained to beneficiaries and can result in a backlash against the perceived preferential treatment of women (Dolan 2009; Turner 1999).

This is, however, not to say that organizations and agencies providing support to people in situations of displacement should not support women or work towards women's empowerment; rather, this needs to happen in a way in which women and men are jointly involved in programmes which reduce their vulnerabilities and increase inclusion and gender equality. In our research in Burundi, Colombia, and Uganda, the gendered shadows of the decades in displacement were in part still very much present in the lives of communities re-building their lives afterwards. The most promising interventions were those of working with men and with women to jointly address these issues, but also other tensions such as between generations, mindful of the intersectional complexities of gender and conscious of local dynamics. However, in engaging with men on gender issues, one also needs to be careful of not focusing only on men and leaving out women, as doing so only serves to cement a different, perhaps less violent, form of male dominance and privilege without fundamentally transforming gendered power dynamics (El-Bushra, Naujoks, and Myrttinen 2014; López and Myrttinen 2014; Myrttinen and Nsengiyumva 2014; Naujoks and Myrttinen 2014).

2.2. *Masculinities and vulnerabilities*

Past research on peace and conflict has partly focused on ways in which patriarchal gender norms, and masculinities in particular, can drive conflict. Policy, development, peacebuilding, and academic discourses around gender and conflict have appeared to endorse 'stereotype[d] notions of gender differences which portray men as belligerents or perpetrators of violence while suggesting that women, as an undifferentiated, homogenised group, are either passive victims or peacemakers' (Wright 2014a). This discourse has tended to emphasize women as a 'vulnerable group' and to separate them out for special assistance. This has had negative consequences for men, since it pushes them into the category of 'perpetrator' and renders the notion of *male* vulnerability essentially unimaginable (El-Bushra, Naujoks, and Myrttinen 2014, 7).

In addition to the pressures placed on men, by themselves and others, to live up to expectations in conflict-affected situations, dominant norms of masculine strength can, seemingly paradoxically, increase men's and boys' vulnerability. The expectation in some societies, especially for younger men, to prove their masculinity by resorting to violence to defend their honour is part of the reason for disproportionately high levels of violent deaths among young men (UNODC 2011). These expectations are also implicit in assumptions that 'able-bodied, military-aged' civilian men are potential combatants and thus somehow assumed to be less worthy of protection by international and national legal norms (see also Jones 2000; Myrttinen 2003).[4]

In some post-war settings, men of a certain age and class, such as motorcycle taxi drivers in Sierra Leone, Liberia, and some other sub-Saharan contexts, are assumed wholesale to be ex-combatants, which can lead to them becoming targets of 'revenge' violence by community members (Menzel 2011). Similarly, in our interviews in Burundi, young, lower class men from poorer districts of Bujumbura reported blanket suspicions of security forces against men considered to be ex-combatants (Myrttinen and Nsengiyumva 2014), while in Colombia, as in other Latin American contexts, young, urban poor men (and to a lesser extent women) suspected of being members of armed groups or gangs have been targeted by security forces and vigilantes as part of often-deadly 'social cleansing' operations (López and Myrttinen 2014). Thus, the assumption that certain men may be or have been militarized and violent can increase their vulnerability, thereby again complicating notions of militarized masculinities being hegemonic across conflict-affected societies.

In addition to the immediate dangers of direct physical harm and death resulting from notions of masculinity, other forms of vulnerability also linked to these norms and expectations may be less visible but possibly more pervasive. In our research on Syrian refugee communities in Lebanon, many of whom originate from rural areas or poorer suburbs of cities in Syria, where men enjoyed greater mobility and economic opportunities than women, expectations of masculinity added to their vulnerability. Displaced Syrian women have in part been adapting more dynamically by making arrangements for their children's schooling, and for food and jobs, as well as accessing health care services (Harvey, Garwood, and El-Masri 2013).

Men, on the other hand, often struggle to find employment, and are vulnerable to abuse and harassment by host communities, living under the constant fear of potentially being sent back to Syria (Khattab and Myrttinen forthcoming). Based on our observations, men were also far less likely than women to access health care and support services, in part due to dominant gender norms of male 'toughness'. In addition to this, expectations of men to be breadwinners means they are expected to be engaging in (or looking for) casual labour opportunities when health care centres are open. Furthermore, the fact that health centres are mostly feminized spaces and most nurses are women, may, based on our observations, act as a barrier for men both to accessing the services and to accepting advice from health care staff. Thus, due to dominant notions of 'strong' masculinity, the men and boys in question are in fact, in certain ways, in a situation of greater vulnerability than the women are.

Furthermore, many of the Syrian refugee men and boys we researched faced a high level of physical insecurity in their countries of refuge. Our research in Lebanon, for instance, highlighted men's mobility restrictions because of fears of being stopped by Lebanese police or army without valid ID and residency papers and subsequently being detained or potentially deported (Khattab and Myrttinen forthcoming). Many Syrian refugee women and girls have had to take on more responsibilities because of men's limited mobility, which impacts them in the sense that they feel their 'femininity' is being compromised, but also impacts family and community relations as a whole, as men's traditional bread-winning and decision-making roles are shifting towards women (Harvey, Garwood, and El-Masri 2013).

Among the more researched forms of conflict-affected vulnerabilities of men and boys is that of SGBV against men and boys. While it had long been a taboo in affected societies, and often still is, it has in recent years been increasingly researched by humanitarian agencies and academia (see for example CARE 2012; Carpenter 2006; Christian et al. 2011; Dolan 2010; Jones and Del Zotto 2002; Leiby 2009; Sivakumaran 2005, 2007; Stemple 2009; Watson 2014). Sexual and gender-based violence against men and boys is often mainly about power and dominance, and the violence can take a range of different forms and meanings depending on the political, cultural, socio-economic, physical, and temporal setting (Drumond 2015 and Myrttinen 2015). One of the most common aims among the different 'messages' conveyed through sexual violence, especially in male rape, is the undermining of the victim's gender and sexual identity, to 'feminize' or 'homosexualize' heterosexual male identities (Dolan 2010; Sivakumaran 2005; Zarkov 2001).

The highly traumatic experience of SGBV affects survivors, their families, and their communities for years afterwards, especially as many feel unable to talk about it given personal and societal expectations of male strength, and misunderstandings of the implications of male-to-male rape for sexuality (Watson 2014). The medical aftercare required is unaffordable for many survivors and when seeking it, men in some societies risk accusations of being homosexual, and thus legal consequences (El-Bushra, Naujoks, and Myrttinen 2014). There is often still a fundamental lack of understanding of SGBV against men in the health, humanitarian, and security sectors, starting with the absence of comprehension of the distinction between consensual and non-consensual sexual relations between men, or understanding that men can become victims of sexual violence. Some of the support which has been set up for female survivors of SGBV has not been accessible to male survivors, as these funds and support are regarded as intended for women only.[5]

In addition to the assault aimed at the sexual and gender identity of the victim, male survivors of SGBV often face severe physical and psychological consequences. Among these may be physical injuries which mean that they are not able to undertake manual labour, which in many conflict-affected situations is the main form of work available. Furthermore, survivors often retreat into themselves, not feeling able to live up to expectations of taking on social responsibilities in the family and community. The continuing emotional and physical trauma and the undermining of their personal and societal gender identities often lead to intense frustration, depression, and withdrawal, and potentially to destructive behaviour, including substance abuse, possibly domestic violence, and suicide (Dolan 2010; Myrttinen, Naujoks, and El-Bushra 2014). One of the main reasons why SGBV against men and boys 'works' so effectively in under-mining survivors' selves is that it thus directly strikes at multiple levels at what it in many societies means to 'be a man' – to be able to protect oneself, one's family, and one's community; to be a breadwinner; to partake in the leadership of the family and community; and to not seek help or support.

2.3. Non-heterosexual masculinities

Sexual and gender minorities (SGM), and their roles, agency, and vulnerabilities in both conflict and post-conflict periods are often wholly absent from gender in peacebuilding discourses and practice (Myrttinen, Naujoks, and El-Bushra 2014). Conflict-affected situations are often highly precarious periods for LGBTI individuals and communities, especially if their position in society is already vulnerable due to dominant, often violently heteronormative norms. They may face increased harassment and exclusion as 'unwanted others'; their loyalty to the nation or state (or membership therein) may be called into question based on their sexuality; and anti-LGBTI mobilization may go hand in hand with more general mobilizations of violent intolerance under the guise of patriotism.[6]

Both in conflict and afterwards, state and non-state armed groups may often be engaged in policing conservative, heterosexual gender norms, violently targeting LGBTI communities (López and Myrttinen 2014; Myrttinen, Khattab, and Maydaa forthcoming; Naujoks and Myrttinen 2014).[7] LGBTI persons are often susceptible to harassment, abuse, extortion, sexual exploitation, sexualized violence, and abuse by security forces, informal violent groups, and individuals, especially in environments such as barracks, police stations, prisons and detention centres, refugee and IDP camps, and border facilities. State and non-state actors may often violently police 'deviant' sexual and gender behaviour among their troops but also among civilian populations, as has been the case in Colombia but also in Iraq and Syria (Centro Nacional de Memoria Histórica

2015; IGLHRC 2014). In some cases, their sexual orientation and gender identity and subsequent persecution may be one of the reasons for displacement. Trans and intersex people are often particularly targeted as they most visibly transgress binary gender norms, while men and women not deemed 'masculine' or 'feminine' enough (even if they do not necessarily self-identify as LGBTI) can be subject to extreme violence, including SGBV and death.

In addition to direct violence, the stigma or lack of understanding can lead to particular vulnerabilities, for instance in accessing services or relief. The particular types of vulnerabilities faced by sexual and gender minorities are often overlooked in humanitarian relief efforts, although the situation is slowly improving (Knight and Sollom 2012; Naujoks and Myrttinen 2014; Naujoks 2016; UNHCR 2015). In Lebanon, for example, Syrian LGBTI refugees have been at times unable or unwilling to access services available to them in the Bekaa Valley, as doing so might reveal their sexual orientation and gender identity to other refugees, potentially endangering them. Local NGOs together with the United Nations High Commissioner for Refugees (UNHCR) have therefore assisted in relocating them to the safer environment of Beirut (Myrttinen, Khattab, and Maydaa forthcoming).

The experiences of Syrian LGBTI refugees in Lebanon in part echo some of the broader problems and vulnerabilities faced by other refugees, but are in part exacerbated by their SOGI status (Myrttinen, Khattab, and Maydaa forthcoming). Many of our respondents reported experiencing harassment (including sexual harassment), insults, and violence at the hands of Syrian state forces, armed groups, and also the Lebanese General Security Forces (*Sûreté Générale* – responsible for border and immigration control). Some had had their documents confiscated by Syrian forces, leaving them in legal limbo in Lebanon. Common problems raised by our respondents and shared by other refugees regardless of their SOGI status included facing harassment and open resentment from the Lebanese population, struggling to pay extortionate rents, lack of documentation or unclear legal status, difficulties in finding employment, and lack of knowledge about and access to services (Myrttinen, Khattab, and Maydaa forthcoming). As with gendered vulnerabilities more broadly, other factors interact with sexual orientation and gender identity in determining possibilities of agency. Higher economic status and education, access to social patronage networks, and the ability to access and reside in more cosmopolitan areas, as well as being seen by others as 'less visibly' LGBTI (or 'less visibly Syrian/refugee') all served to reduce vulnerability at the hand of the security forces, members of the Lebanese public, and other refugees but also within the LGBTI scene (Myrttinen, Khattab, and Maydaa forthcoming).

Nonetheless, due to the persistent invisibility of SOGI issues in humanitarian aid, peacebuilding, and development policy, training, and implementation guidelines, staff may often overlook these concerns, an issue often compounded by unease and prejudice surrounding these issues. This is also partly due to a focus on heterosexual nuclear family units in relief efforts, including for the analysis and distribution of relief services – a heteronormative approach that can lead to SGM being overlooked. By way of example, after floods destroyed villages in Sunsari, Nepal, in 2008, SGM families received only half the relief given to other families, forcing some SGM to relocate to India and take up sex work in order to survive (Knight and Sollom 2012). Similar shortcomings of exclusion and neglect of SGM needs and rights are likely to apply to peacebuilding, development, and access to justice and security, even in countries such as Nepal with progressive policies on these issues (Naujoks 2016; Naujoks and Myrttinen 2014).

As with gender identities more broadly, socio-economic class and other identity factors play a significant role in the opportunities, vulnerabilities, and social acceptance for SGM. Those in urban areas may benefit from greater anonymity and economic opportunities than those in rural areas. Those who are part of a higher socio-economic group may be less vulnerable economically or able to 'buy' a degree of acceptance through patronage networks, a pattern visible in Colombia as much as in Lebanon (López and Myrttinen 2014; Khattab and Myrttinen 2014). However, this can also be the other way around. Based on anecdotal evidence from Nepal, social acceptance may be higher among the lower castes, who have less status to lose and more scope to be themselves without being subjected to the same labelling, prejudices, and distrust they might encounter in the cities (Naujoks and Myrttinen 2014).

Same-sex or SGM couples may furthermore face particular stigma and obstacles in seeking support in the event of domestic violence, as this may be considered by some in the community as 'betraying' an SGM community which is already facing discrimination and prejudice – but at the same time might put the person reporting the violence into a double bind if non-heterosexual ways of living together are criminalized (Khattab and Myrttinen 2014). Furthermore, SGM relationships can also reproduce strong patriarchal structures of dominance which disadvantage or marginalize the subordinate partner regardless of their sex. In addition to the social stigma, there can be legal limitations as not all legal systems even recognize SGBV or domestic violence as also happening to men, or between men.

3. Conclusion

Although men, boys, and the masculinities they enact are in central roles in conflict-affected situations, the gender, peace, and security discourse has paid comparatively little attention to them. When men and boys are addressed, it is mostly as perpetrators of violence, and on occasion as actors for positive change. In terms of examining men and boys as agents of violence, the notion of violent, military/militarized masculinities being hegemonic has become increasingly commonplace. We have argued here that this needs to be re-examined and that the notion of hegemonic masculinities needs to be re-articulated in more nuanced ways, allowing for the complexity of military/militarized masculinities, and of the differing ways in which societies view the relationship among violence, militarization, and masculinity. We have also argued that the scope of studying masculinities in conflict-affected situations needs to be broadened to go beyond merely examining the violent masculinities. We have sought to look beyond some of the more usual narratives, drawing on field research we conducted in various settings.

The mainstream literature and programming on gender, peace, and security has tended in the past to be dominated by representations of a narrow binary: women as powerless victims and men as perpetrators of violence. While the role of men and masculinities has to some (limited but increasing) extent been researched in the context of violent and armed conflict, much less attention has been focused on researching it in relation to peacebuilding. In the field of peacebuilding, men's attitudes, values, and behaviours have in fact rarely been considered from an intersectional and relational *gender* perspective (Wright 2014b). A paradoxical result of the dominant, narrow focus on masculinities, violence, and militarization is that it may end up reinforcing what it seeks to critique and dismantle, namely that being a man means to be violent, as alternative ways of being a man are not given space in the discourses. However, an uncritical and mainly male-focused embrace of 'men and boys as actors of positive change' also runs the risk of further bolstering male privilege. Through more nuanced research, policies, and programming, existing non-violent alternatives to being men, women, trans, and intersex persons can be articulated and supported.

We started with a questioning of the rapidly proliferating use of the concept of hegemonic masculinities in the conflict and peacebuilding sector, be it in academia, policy, or programming, arguing against a simplistic equating of hegemonic masculinities with violence and militarization, and also arguing for more context specificity. The examples we examined of thwarted masculinities, of conflict-affected male vulnerabilities, and of the positions of those not conforming to dominant notions of sexual orientation and gender identity are all linked to locally dominant norms of what it means to be a man. These will be different for different men, depending on age, class, dis-/ability, marital status, urban/rural setting, and so on, but also dependent on the situation – differences which need to be factored in when approaching questions of conflict-affected masculinities. In spite of the particular differences between, say, rural Burundi or the streets of Beirut, what does appear as a general pattern, though, are the immense and varied costs of these dominant notions of masculinity upon men and women in conflict-affected societies.

The increasing policy interest in 'engaging with men and boys as actors of change', evident for example in UN Security Council Resolution 2242 (2015), is both a risk and a chance for critical, transformative approaches to masculinities. The risk is that the phrase will remain just that, added on in the way that '…and women and girls' has too often been simply added on. The chance, on the other hand, is to use this opening for truly transformative work, with men, women, and those not identifying with gender binaries, to tackle harmful, dominant notions of masculinities and femininities. This, however, requires deeper, in-depth understanding of the particular dynamics at play. Here, we would see a clear calling for more dialogue and interaction between academia and 'practitioners', with both sides bringing their tools and experiences to the table, and re-thinking conflict-affected masculinities and femininities beyond narrow simplifications. This would open new areas for bringing critical masculinities from the conceptual area of study into practical programming of peacebuilding organizations and interventions, questioning one-dimensional understandings of what it means to be a man, and creating new spaces for new masculinities.

Notes

1. We differentiate here between military masculinities (i.e. masculinities inculcated, constructed, and performed in military and military-like institutions) and militarized masculinities (i.e. masculinities which have been actively militarized, through one's own volition and/or via outside actors). While there is considerable overlap, they are not identical: civilian, right-wing, 'lone wolf' assassins often display more militarized forms of masculinities than, for example, the military masculinity of a logistics clerk in a state army.
2. The degree to which 'hegemonic masculinities' has gained currency among practitioners working on violent male behaviour was highlighted at a major international symposium on

masculinities in New Delhi in 2014 where the term was used by a wide range of presenters interchangeably with violent (and militarized) forms of masculinity in situations as divergent as the Israeli occupation in Palestine; young, urban underclass gang members in El Salvador; or middle-aged, upper-middle-class Bengali men.

3. The research was conducted in Burundi and Colombia in 2013, in Lebanon 2014 and 2015, in Nepal in 2013–2014, and in Uganda in 2012–2013. For the in-depth findings and more detail on the research methodology, see El-Bushra, Naujoks, and Myrttinen (2014), Khattab and Myrttinen (2014; 2016), López and Myrttinen (2014), Myrttinen, Naujoks, and El-Bushra (2014), Myrttinen and Nsengiyumva (2014) and Naujoks and Myrttinen (2014).

4. This assumption has been evident in internationally brokered local ceasefires in Syria, in which women and children have been allowed to leave besieged areas, but not 'men of military age'. This criterion of separation was also used in the 1995 Srebrenica massacre, in which around 8000 Bosnian Muslim men and boys were killed.

5. Interviews, 2012–2013, Uganda. See also Eriksson Baaz and Stern (2013).

6. For recent examples, see the homophobic undercurrents in the debates about Chelsea Manning in the USA; or the nationalist anti-gay mobilizations in Armenia, Georgia, Greece, and Russia in 2013–2014; and, with slightly different dynamics at play, the recent pushes to introduce religiously motivated anti-LGBTI legislation across different parts of the globe. Conversely, right-wing groups in Northern Europe have also sought to instrumentalize LGBTI rights in their xeno- and Islamophobic narratives.

7. Although there is a tendency for armed state and non-state actors, regardless of their ideology, to instil heteronormative versions of appropriate male and female behaviour, one may also find openness to diverse practices; for example, the first gay marriage in the Philippines organized by the Maoist New People's Army (see, for example, Alburo 2011; López and Myrttinen 2014).

Disclosure statement

No potential conflict of interest was reported by the authors.

References

Alburo, K., 2011. Brothers, lovers and revolution: Negotiating military masculinity and homosexual identity in a revolutionary movement in the Philippines. *Asia-Pacific Social Science Review* 11, no. 2: 27–42.

Barrett, F., 1996. The organizational construction of hegemonic masculinity: The case of the U.S. navy. *Gender, Work & Organization* 3, no. 3: 129–42. doi:10.1111/gwao.1996.3.issue-3

Beasley, C., 2008. Rethinking hegemonic masculinity in a globalizing world. *Men and Masculinities* 11, no. 1: 86–103. doi:10.1177/1097184X08315102

Belkin, A. 2012. *Bring me men: Military masculinity and the benign facade of American empire, 1898-2001*. Oxford: Oxford University Press.

CARE. 2012. *Roco Kwo: Mid-term review*. Kampala: CARE International in Uganda.

Carpenter, R.C., 2006. Recognizing gender-based violence against civilian men and boys in conflict situations. *Security Dialogue* 37, no. 1: 83–103. doi:10.1177/0967010606064139

Centro Nacional de Memoria Histórica. 2015. *Aniquilar la diferencia - Lesbianas, Gays, Bisexuales y Transgeneristas en el Marco del Conflicto Armado Colombiano*. Bogotá: Centro Nacional de Memoria Histórica.

Chisholm, A., 2014. The silenced and indispensable: Gurkhas in private military security companies. *International Feminist Journal of Politics* 16, no. 1: 26–47. doi:10.1080/14616742.2013.781441

Christian, M., O. Safari, P. Ramazani, G. Burnham, and N. Glass, 2011. Sexual and gender based violence against men in the democratic republic of Congo: Effects on survivors, their families and the community. *Medicine, Conflict and Survival* 27, no. 4: 227–46. doi:10.1080/ 13623699.2011.645144

Confortini, C., 2006. Galtung, violence, and gender: The case for a peace studies/feminism alliance. *Peace & Change* 31, no. 3: 333–67. doi:10.1111/j.1468-0130.2006.00378.x

Connell, R.W. 1987. *Gender and power: Society, the person and sexual politics*. Cambridge: Polity Press.

Connell, R.W. 1995. *Masculinities*. Los Angeles: University of California Press.

De Silva, J. 2005. *Globalization, terror & the shaming of the nation: Constructing local masculinities in a Sri Lankan village*. Crewe: Trafford Publishers.

Dolan, C. 2001. *Collapsing Masculinities and Weak States – a case study of northern Uganda*. (unpublished).

Dolan, C. 2009. *Social torture: The case of northern Uganda 1986–2006*. Oxford: Berghahn Books.

Dolan, C. 2010. *War is not yet over: Community perceptions of sexual violence and its underpinnings in eastern DRC*. London: International Alert.

Dolan, C. 2002. Collapsing masculinities and weak states – a case study of northern Uganda. In *Masculinities matter! men, gender and development*, ed. F. Cleaver, London: Zed Books.

Drumond, P. 2015. Embodied battlefields - uncovering sexual violence against men in war theaters. Unpublished paper presented at workshop on "Sexual Violence Against Men during Conflicts: Bridging the Gap between Theory and Practice, February26-27, Geneva: Graduate Institute.

Duncanson, C. 2013. *Forces for good? Military masculinities and peacebuilding in Afghanistan and Iraq*. London: Palgrave Macmillan.

Dworkin, S., A. Hatcher, C. Colvin, and D. Peacock, 2012. Impact of a gender-transformative HIV and antiviolence program on gender ideologies and masculinities in Two Rural, South African communities. *Men and Masculinities* 16, no. 2: 181–202. doi:10.1177/ 1097184X12469878

El-Bushra, J. 2012. *Gender in peacebuilding: Taking Stock*. London: International Alert.

El-Bushra, J., J. Naujoks, and H. Myrttinen. 2014. *Renegotiating the ideal society: gender in peacebuilding in Uganda*. London: International Alert.

El-Bushra, J., and I. Sahl. 2005. *Cycles of violence: Gender relations and armed conflict*. Nairobi: ACORD.

Eriksson Baaz, M., and M. Stern, 2009. Why do soldiers rape? Masculinity, violence, and sexuality in the armed forces in the Congo (DRC). *International Studies Quarterly* 53, no. 2: 495–518. doi:10.1111/isqu.2009.53.issue-2

Eriksson Baaz, M., and M. Stern. 2013. *Sexual violence as a weapon of war? Perceptions, prescriptions, problems in the Congo and beyond*. London: Zed Books.

Gibbs, A., R. Jewkes, Y. Sikweyiya, and S. Willan, 2015. Reconstructing masculinity? A qualitative evaluation of the stepping stones and creating futures interventions in urban informal settlements in South Africa. *Culture, Health & Sexuality: an International Journal for Research, Intervention and Care* 17, no. 2: 208–22. doi:10.1080/13691058.2014.966150

Haaland, T. 2012. Friendly war-fighters and invisible women: Perceptions of gender and masculinities in the Norwegian armed forces on missions abroad. In *Making gender, making war. Violence, military and peacekeeping practices*, eds. E. Svedberg, and A. Kronsell, 63–75. London: Routledge.

Harvey, C., R. Garwood, and R. El-Masri. 2013. *Shifting sands: Changing gender roles among refugees in Lebanon*. Beirut: Oxfam and Abaad Resource Centre for Gender Equality.

Hearn, J. 1998. *The violences of men*. London: Sage Publications.

Higate, P. 2003. *Military masculinities: Identity and the state*. London/Santa Barbara: Praeger Publishers.

Higate, P., 2012. Martial races and enforcement masculinities of the global south: Weaponising Fijian, Chilean, and Salvadoran Postcoloniality in the mercenary sector. *Globalizations* 9: 35–52. doi:10.1080/14747731.2012.627717

Hoffman, D. 2011. *The war machines: Young men and violence in sierra Leone and Liberia*. Durham: Duke University Press.

IGLHRC. 2014. *When coming out is a death sentence - persecution of LGBT Iraqis*. New York: IGLHRC.

Ignatieff, M. 1998. *The warrior's honour – ethnic war and the modern consciousness*. London: Random House.

Jones, A., 2000. Gendercide and genocide. *Journal of Genocide Research* 2, no. 2: 185–211. doi:10.1080/713677599

Jones, A., and A. Del Zotto. 2002. Male-on-male sexual violence in wartime: Human rights' last taboo? Paper presented to the Annual Convention of the International Studies Association (ISA), March 23-27, New Orleans

Kabachnik, P., M. Grabowska, J. Regulska, B. Mitchneck, and O. Mayorova. 2013. Traumatic masculinities: the gendered geographies of georgian idps from abkhazia. gender, Place & Culture: 20, no. 6: 773-793. doi: 10.1080/0966369X.2012.716402

Kesmaecker-Wissing, M., and A. Pagot. 2015. *Driven apart: How repeated displacement changes family dynamics in eastern DRC*. Geneva: Internal Displacement Monitoring Centre.

Khattab, L., and H. Myrttinen. 2014. *Gender, security and SSR in Lebanon*. Beirut: International Alert.

Khattab, L., and H. Myrttinen. forthcoming. '*Most men prefer to go back home... '– Gender and the dynamics of joining/not-joining armed groups in Syria*. London: International Alert.

Kimmel, M. 1987. *Changing men: New directions in research on men and masculinity*. New York: Sage Publishers.

Kirby, P., and L. Shepherd, 2016. Reintroducing women, peace and security. *International Affairs* 92, no. 2: 249–54. doi:10.1111/inta.2016.92.issue-2

Knight, K., and R. Sollom. 2012. Making disaster risk reduction and relief programmes LGBTI inclusive: Examples from Nepal. *Humanitarian Exchange Magazine*, no. 55.

Kronsell, A., 2005. Gendered practices in institutions of hegemonic masculinity - Reflections from feminist standpoint theory. *International Feminist Journal of Politics* 7, no. 2: 280–98. doi:10.1080/14616740500065170

Leiby, M., 2009. Wartime sexual violence in guatemala and Peru. *International Studies Quarterly* 53, no. 2: 445–68. doi:10.1111/isqu.2009.53.issue-2

López, D., and H. Myrttinen. 2014. *Re-examining identities and power: Gender and peacebuilding in Colombia*. London: International Alert.

Martin, P.Y., 1998. Why can't a man be more like a woman? Reflections on Connell's masculinities. *Gender & Society* 12, no. 4: 472–74. doi:10.1177/089124398012004008

Menzel, A., 2011. Between ex-combatantization and opportunities for peace: The double-edged qualities of motorcycle-taxi driving in urban postwar Sierra Leone. *Africa Today* 58, no. 2: 97–127. doi:10.2979/africatoday.58.2.97

Messner, M., 1990. When bodies are weapons: Masculinity and violence in sport. *International Review for the Sociology of Sport* 25, no. 3: 203–18. doi:10.1177/101269029002500303urn of the millennium and persistently

Moore, H. 1994. *A passion for difference*. London: Polity Press.

Myrttinen, H., 2003. Disarming masculinities. *Disarmament Forum* 4, no. 2003: 37–46.

Myrttinen, H. 2010. Histories of Violence, States of Denial: Militias, Martial Arts and Masculinities in Timor-Leste. Unpublished Ph.D. Thesis, University of KwaZulu-Natal.

Myrttinen, H. 2015. Building a heteronormative peace? Examining unstated gender assumptions in peacebuilding programming. Presentation at the International Studies Association Annual Conference 2015, New Orleans, USA.

Myrttinen, H., L. Khattab, and C. Maydaa. forthcoming. "Trust no one, beware of everyone" – Vulnerabilities of LGBTI refugees in Lebanon. In *A gendered approach to the Syrian refugee crisis*, eds. J. Freedman, Z. Kivilcim, and N Baklacıoğlu, London: Routledge.

Myrttinen, H., J. Naujoks, and J. El-Bushra. 2014. *Rethinking gender in peacebuilding*. London: International Alert.

Myrttinen, H., and P.C. Nsengiyumva. 2014. *Rebuilding dignified lives: Gender in peacebuilding in Burundi*. London: International Alert.

Naujoks, J. 2016. *Building Back Better or Restoring Inequalities? Gender and conflict sensitivity in the response to Nepal's 2015 Earthquakes.* International Alert: London.

Naujoks, J., and H. Myrttinen. 2014. *Reassessing gender norms after conflict: Gender and peacebuilding in Nepal.* London: International Alert.

Reychler, L., and A. Stellamans, 2003. Peacebuilding leaders and spoilers. *Cahiers Internationale Betrekkingen En Vredesonderzoek* 21, no. 1: 1–49.

Sivakumaran, S., 2005. Male/male rape and the 'Taint' of homosexuality. *Human Rights Quarterly* 27, no. 4: 1274–306. doi:10.1353/hrq.2005.0053

Sivakumaran, S., 2007. Sexual violence against men in armed conflict. *European Journal of International Law* 18, no. 2: 253–76. doi:10.1093/ejil/chm013

Steger, M. 2001. Peacebuilding and nonviolence: Gandhi's perspective on power. In *Peace, conflict, and violence: peace psychology for the 21st century*, eds. D. J. Christie, R. V. Wagner, and D. A. Winter, Englewood Cliffs: Prentice-Hall.

Stemple, L., 2009. Male rape and human rights. *Hastings Law Journal* 60, no. 2009: 605–47.

Tidy, J., 2015. Gender, dissenting subjectivity and the contemporary military peace movement in body of war. *International Feminist Journal of Politics* 17, no. 3: 454–72. doi:10.1080/14616742.2014.967128

Titunik, R., 2008. The myth of the macho military. *Polity* 40, no. 2: 137–63. doi:10.1057/palgrave.polity.2300090

Turner, S. 1999. *Angry young men in camps: Gender, age and class relations among Burundian refugees in Tanzania.* Geneva: UNHCR Centre for Documentation and Research.

Udasmoro, W., H. Myrttinen, and R. Kunz. forthcoming. *Preachers, Pirates and Peacebuilding – Examining Non-Violent Hegemonic Masculinities in Aceh.*

UNHCR. 2015. *Protecting persons with diverse sexual orientations and gender identities – A global report on UNHCR's efforts to protect lesbian, gay, bisexual, transgender, and intersex asylum-seekers and refugees.* Geneva: United Nations High Commissioner For Refugees.

UNODC. 2011. *2011 global study on homicide – trends, contexts, data.* Vienna: United Nations Office on Drugs and Crime.

Vigh, H. 2006. *Navigating terrains of war - youth and soldiering in Guinea-Bissau.* Oxford: Berghahn Books.

Watson, C. 2014. *Preventing and responding to sexual and domestic violence against men: A guidance note for security sector institutions.* Geneva: DCAF.

Wetherell, M., and N. Edley, 1999. Negotiating hegemonic masculinity: Imaginary positions and psycho-discursive practices. *Feminism & Psychology* 9, no. 3: 335–56. doi:10.1177/0959353599009003012

Whitworth, S. 2004. *Men, militaries, and UN peacekeeping: A gendered analysis.* Boulder, CO: Lynne Rienner Publishers.

Women, U.N. 2015. *Preventing conflict, transforming justice, securing the peace – A global study on the implementation of united nations security council resolution 1325.* New York: UN Women.

Wright, H. 2014a. *Masculinities, conflict and peacebuilding: Perspectives on men through a gender lens.* London: Saferworld.

Wright, H., 2014b. *Addressing notions of masculinity that drive conflict.* London: Saferworld. http://www.saferworld.org.uk/news-and-views/comment/156-addressing-notions-of-masculinity-that-drive-conflict (accessed January 17 2016).

Zarkov, D. 2001. The body of the other man: Sexual violence and the construction of masculinity, sexuality and ethnicity in Croatian media. In *Victims, Perpetrators or actors? Gender, armed conflict and political violence*, eds. C.O.N. Moser, and F. Clark, 69–82. London: Zed Books.

Clients, contractors, and the everyday masculinities in global private security

Amanda Chisholm 🆔

ABSTRACT

This article explores the intimate relationships between the client and the security contractor. It draws upon autoethnography to bring into focus the client/contractor encounters and demonstrate how such encounters (re)shape the marginal and hegemonic men/ masculinities of the security industry – masculinities which work to legitimize not only who and what are appropriate security providers but also how value/valuation of security is understood and practised. As such it contributes to the broader debates about gender and war by (1) demonstrating how the researcher is always embedded in and shaped by the research she produces; and (2) by bringing to the fore the multitude of masculinities, beyond the hegemonic militarized, that emerge in private security markets.

Militarism, markets, and everyday gender encounters

Between 2008 and 2010, I made two trips to Kabul, Afghanistan, to research private security contractors in conflict zones. At the time I had just finished some graduate research on private military and security companies (PMSCs) and was curious to find out more about the men (and sometimes women) who work in the global armed security industry. During both stays in Kabul I received protection from a variety of security contractors, of nationalities including British, South African, Afghan, and Nepalese.

I remember vividly the first time I arrived in Kabul. As I and the other passengers disembarked the plane on an old tarmac I was a bit confused as to which door of the dusty small building to enter. I tightened the scarf around my head and made sure none of my hair was sticking out. I looked to the other passengers and watched how they were walking and what they were wearing. The white women, of which there were few, walked confidently up to the building and into a queue that was beginning to form with the other passengers. I followed these women with caution but tried to act confidently, as if I had flown into hostile environments numerous times. I politely smiled at the Afghan immigration officer as I handed over my passport and then quickly withdrew the smile. Did I smile too widely? Was I unintentionally being flirty? I checked again to make sure my hair was tightly tucked under my headscarf and looked around at the other passengers, through immigration now, waiting for their luggage. They were mostly white men, dressed in desert-coloured cargo pants, and polo shirts with puffer jackets – the informal dress of the white security contractor, I would later find out. They, like the female passengers, appeared both casual and annoyed at how long it was taking to get their luggage. I was completely out of my element and became concerned everyone could see this. My insides were churning and I was feeling nauseated. What was I doing in a conflict zone? I calmly walked up to the luggage carousel and quietly waited for my luggage as I checked once more to make sure my hair was tucked into my headscarf.

These initial feelings about my own insecurity and how I then attempted to *perform* a calm female academic who could be taken seriously did not completely go away. I needed to feel safe, not only to come across as credible, as someone who could be taken seriously, but also so I could physically do the research I wanted to do in the city. As I've written elsewhere, these private security contractors played a vital role in helping me feel safe (Chisholm 2016). They appeared calm and confident in everyday life in Kabul. I wanted to feel this way and so I listened to them, watched them, and tried to comply with their security advice.

In security briefings I listened to these men using technocratic language like 'risk mitigation' and talking through various strategies to avoid *making contact* with danger- ous people who lurked outside the compound. I watched them monitor the armed local contractors who stood in front of the compound where we lived. Through these interactions I was repeatedly reminded that I did not have the security knowledge and the *ground truths* to handle my own security, truths that come through years of military service in dangerous places.

Despite spending five years training as a military medic with the Canadian military, I never experienced combat – I was never on the front line and so I had no relevant previous skills or experience to refer to. Such ground truths, as Tidy (2016) reminds us, are not objective but act as authority claims to knowledge of war. These truths are highly gendered. They reinforce authority rooted in *boots on the ground* experience through the embodied masculine model of the combat soldier (Tidy 2016). My female- sexed body and my lack of combat experience prevented me from obtaining such truths. I could only ever be a friendly ally of these contractors, one who could empathize immediately with the military culture, but could not fully participate as a security expert.

I recall one morning hearing an explosion and then some small bursts of gunfire. At the time I was finishing up a field note entry from the previous night. Sharing an office space with one of the security contractors living in the compound with me, I was amazed at how he knew the type of gun that made those sounds and the direction the shots were coming from. He quickly jumped up and began directing other guards, who were already performing security drills of locking down the compound we were staying in. I followed him up to the rooftop of the compound where we both could get a better look at what was happening outside. A few streets down we saw a plume of smoke coming from a house. He said it was the United Nations (UN) guesthouse. I was cautious and curious as I absorbed what he was saying. I stayed a few feet behind him and watched as he calmly and casually approached the rooftop outer wall and peered over. Suddenly we heard another bang. I instantly ducked. He looked back at me and laughed. That's only kids with firecrackers, he said. Shaken, I quickly retreated into the house. I was amazed at his ability to discern the source of all these noise bursts. They all sounded the same to me.

His demonstration of knowledge about firepower and military tactics alongside the calm demeanor and habitual drills set immediately into motion reminded me who the security experts were and what my place as the female client was – the one who complies, who looks on with awe at the tactics and abilities. It is through these everyday encounters, which shaped my understanding of security and the role these men played in making my life safe, that my gender analysis begins.

Autoethnography in critical gender studies of global security

To date, any self-reflections within feminist and critical literatures on private security industry remain absent. Yet it is these autoethnographic reflections that show how valuations of military masculinities and security are constructed through everyday gendered performances. As such, autoethnography offers an important methodological intervention into how knowledge about the industry is produced through these gendered encounters. It turns the analytical gaze onto the researcher who is a part of the social she researches. It touches upon feelings, observations, and the messiness of the field she constructs in her knowledge claims about security.

The autoethnographic reflections throughout this article are heavily indebted to the intellectual work of feminist poststructuralist who see gender and security not as ontological givens, but produced through repetitive performances (Butler 1990; Shepherd 2008; Higate and Henry 2010; Wadley 2010). Security, as demonstrated in the above reflections, came through repetitive performativities of particular military masculinities. The regular drills, the technocratic language, the immediate response to incidents all told me these militarized men were confident and were in charge.

I also owe much intellectual credit to the feminist autoethnography writings before mine – those that interweave the vulnerabilities and fluidities of the researcher self into the social that they research (Taber 2005; Dauphinee 2013a, 2013b) – and to black feminist thinkers (Collins 2009; Griffin 2012) who continue to understand writing as a political, emancipatory, hopeful, emotional, and complicated process. These writings combined have all argued for the importance of listening and giving voice to the experiences of women who are often written out of global politics writings, and highlight the politics that underpin their racialized and gendered marginal status. They demand a type of writing that brings to the fore the 'murmurs' and the 'silences' that are a part of global politics (Dauphinee 2013a).

Autoethnography of everyday encounters also helps us get at the ways in which the militarized field speaks to theory (Baker et al. 2016). It allows us to be accountable to the research we produce (Gray 2016) as well as how we produce knowledge (Cohn 1987; Enloe 2010). These everyday encounters I opened with and discuss throughout the article are not disconnected from theory – rather, they shape and speak to the ways we draw upon masculinities to understand violence, insecurities, and war (Enloe 2000). These everyday encounters show in concrete ways how the personal is always international and how masculinities and militarism shape both (Enloe 2000, 2011).

Militarism and masculinities have been important concepts for feminists studying gender in global politics. Feminists have understood them as rationales and modes of behaviour that frame how we perform, enact, incite, and evaluate security (Shepherd 2008). Yet masculinities, like security itself, have no ontological given. Rather, inspired by Butler's (1990, 1993) informative work on performativities, feminist international relations (IR) scholars have demonstrated how both security and masculinities remain ambiguous concepts, codes of conduct and broader rationales made meaningful through the language we use to describe them, in different political and social interactions and the practices and performances/performativities of them (Sylvester 1994; Shepherd 2008; Higate and Henry 2010).

Feminist scholars such as Agathangelou and Ling (2009) and Richter-Montpetit (2016) have highlighted that we cannot understand military masculinities solely within the frames of gender, but must also examine how gender intersects with race, sexuality and colonialist. By doing so, these scholars have been able to show how military violence occurs under broader colonial logics of gender. It is these very ambiguities and infinite flexibilities of masculinities, practised through logics of (neo)coloniality, that we as feminists curious about security and violence need to pay attention to. My personal reflections detailed above and the dialogues that are discussed below then cannot be divorced from the broader colonial geopolitics that informs how we understand what security is and are conditioned to look for and to feel, when we are encountering (in)security through the everyday.

Masculinities and security markets

Feminists studying the commercialization and privatization of security have detailed the various masculinities that are brought into neoliberal security markets. Theoretical discussions have talked about how the industry remasculinizes and valourizes traditional notions of masculine security (Stachowitsch 2014, 2013, 2015), how the industry draws upon and reconfigures the global workforce of military labour (Eichler 2014; Chisholm 2015), and how it is rendered intelligible through broader gendered neoliberal and racial projects (Eichler 2013; Joachim and Schneiker 2012; Chisholm 2014a). Empirically focused analysis looks at the on-the-ground operations through a sociological/ethnographic-based inquiry that positions the men of the industry as the main site of inquiry. Scholars such as Higate (2012), Ware (2016), Barker (2009), Chisholm (2014a, 2014b, 2015), and Chisholm and Stachowitsch (2016) use such empirical insights to highlight how the industry categorizes the men (and sometimes women) who work as racialized, gendered, and classed contractors. While this research remains important in understanding the gendered practices of the industry, the ways in which masculinities in the industry are produced through everyday encounters – and the researchers who write about them – remain absent.

This article attempts to address this gap in two important ways. The first is methodological. As mentioned, most research on gender and war by the feminist researcher continues to be written out of the actual analysis. Consequently, we know very little about the ways the everyday remains important in shaping how we as academics think about, empathize with, and write about masculinities in war (Cohn 1987; Enloe 2000, 2010; Dauphinee 2013b). Here I move beyond the self-reflective disclaimers which often briefly appear in the methods sections of articles, to actively engage with Cohn's, Dauphinee's, and Enloe's important works by asking: How does being protected by the very people whom you are researching impact upon the knowledge you produce?

By making commitments to better theorize military masculinities within the market and to autoethnographic methods, this article opens up space to pose these important questions of knowledge production of military masculinities in the neoliberal security era – an era marked by diverse forms of militarisms and masculinities (Henry 2015; Tidy 2015; Richter-Montpetit 2016; Myrttinen 2004). The second contribution is an empirical one. By focusing on the client and contractor relationship, this article is able to consider how hegemonic conceptions of military masculinities change when they collude with neoliberal market logics. This article shows how market value and valuation of security labour, articulated through gendered embodied relations between the client and contractor, are processes that do not always privilege traditional notions of hegemonic masculine security.

Autoethnography and the everyday

Feminists have for a long while reminded us that the everyday is fundamental in shaping experiences of violence and (in)security. They do more than just showcase how IR and global economics impact upon everyday lives: they demonstrate how everyday encounters intellectually shape how we understand gender and war (see for example the works of Cohn 1987; Henry 2015; Tickner 2003; Enloe 2000, 2010, 2011; Ware 2016). I draw upon these feminist insights to demonstrate how conceptualizations of global security practices are, whilst largely unacknowledged, fundamentally rooted in our gendered embodied experiences with the field – broadly defined to include those who engage in the field from 'afar', through mediums such as blogs, websites and secondary sources, and those who engage in dialogue and participatory practices with industry practitioners.

I begin with the everyday. The everyday is understood as a practise of banal activities including consumption practices and daily routines as much as it is a geographic and spatial marker of the ways in which global capital discursively sections off the international from the local (Davies 2006, 2016). These conceptual moves are profoundly gendered and include, for example, the feminization and racialization of work and workers globally (Elias and Roberts 2016). The everyday points to the embodiment of global capital and war. It captures 'the mess, pain and pleasure of everyday life' (Pettman 2003, 158 cited in Elais and Roberts, 2016 790) and how the global comes to bear upon and be constituted through the local (Elias and Roberts 2016).

Foregrounding my own positionalities as both a researcher and client can illuminate how knowledge production about security in the everyday needs to also account for the gendered relations between the researcher (and client) and those she researches. By acknowledging our own implications in and reproductions of gender knowledge as researchers, we can begin to unpack/reorientate the authority claims behind these gendered ground truths – ground truths that, as Tidy reminds us, continue to maintain an unquestioned 'objective' legitimacy for hegemonic conceptions of military masculinities in how we understand and talk about gender and war (Tidy 2016).

I focus on the everyday local processes by which certain masculinities appear dominant, professional, dangerous, or otherwise. I demonstrate how gender positionality matters in the types of research we produce: how we navigate the field and who we have access to, and what language we can use to describe the field experiences directly shaping our research. Locating the researcher as a valid object of study raises important analytical questions: How does the gendered researcher, specifically that one being protected by the very security she seeks to research, impact upon the analysis she makes and the stories she tells about the security industry? What do the masculinities that are marked dangerous, lazy, and insecure tell us about the broader knowledge productions and practices of global security assemblages? Further, what can the marginal masculinities tell us about how such masculinities shape the broader cultural circulation of knowledge about security actors?

Taking these questions seriously means that 'militarized masculinities' is not a concept we apply onto the field, but one that is given meaning and shaped through how we relate to the field – the logics, practices, and subjectivities we empathize and connect with and how we later tell their stories of security (Cohn 1987). Consequently, this article highlights how the masculinities we come to value and to vilify are, in part, a result of our own situated and gendered encounters with the field.

In conversation with other security clients

My own experiences are coupled with dialogues with other men and women who were protected by security contractors. I say dialogues as opposed to interviews because dialogue, as Collins argues, is a method that sees the interview process as productive of knowledge and not an extraction of knowledge by the researcher from the researched (Collins 2009). It therefore immediately accounts for the research process as productive of particular kinds of knowledge – foregrounding both the gender and racial subjectivities of the interviewer/interviewees. During the dialogues, those I conversed with were open to ask questions of me, to elicit my opinions and feelings on the questions I posed to them. I followed the important methodological work of Gunaratnam (2003), and treated the engagement with those interviewed as productive of race and gender, as opposed to understanding these dialogues as a reflection or an empirical fact that supports an already preconceived understanding of what race and gender look like. In many ways my own reflections are echoed in the experiences raised through the conversations, and in some ways they are not. These tensions are not flattened out but given space throughout the article. They show how meaning about security is not created via a straightforward process, but is produced through contradictions.

The security clients I talked to all worked in Kabul for extended periods of time with the UN or commercial construction companies. I was introduced to these people through personal contacts I had made during my time in Kabul and who still remain in the city. These people were all white, western nationals. In total, three men and five women were interviewed. Their names have been changed to protect their anonymity.

The dialogues took place in 2014, four years after my own experiences, ranged from one to two hours, and occurred over Skype. During these sessions I took on a position as a group member but also as an academic concerned with how security practices are experienced by the clients. However, just because I was a member of this group, inasmuch as I shared a commonality of being protected by private security while in Afghanistan, this does not allow me to represent clear, constant, and coherent patterns of being protected. A clear and coherent story of the protected is lacking in part because one does not exist and in part because my own embodiment as an academic will invariably foreclose on accessing different perspectives.

Instead I envisioned my role as self-conscious participant and my understandings emerging not from either the participant or the researcher, but from dialogues (Anderson 2006, 382). In conversations, I openly acknowledged my own position as both an academic and a client who was protected. I used the former identity marker to collectively explore with the interviewee experiences and feelings around sensitive topics such as how racialization informs how we understand what constitutes good security, how we are complicit in this often problematic racial profiling of security contractors, and where our own assumptions were challenged.

This article highlights some of the topics raised in these discussions. It unfolds with a discussion of two archetypes of security providers in Kabul, the Gurkhas and the white westerners. These categories of contractors arose during initial discussions that primarily focused on Gurkha contractors – something I have written extensively about elsewhere (Chisholm 2014a, 2014b, 2015) and was particularly interested in exploring with others. I was curious how others felt about being protected by them, and their value and worth within broader security practices. As to be expected, Gurkha value was understood in relational terms – how they measured against other national/ethic contractors. The categories of security contractors are not as discrete as this article portrays them. They are meant to illuminate the role race and nationhood play in how clients value particular security, and how this valuing is bound up with how the security market places value on these men's labour and skillsets.

The remainder of the article proceeds with the following sections. 'Producing the martial Gurkha and the flawed westerner through everyday encounters' details two relational archetype security contractors who were described and categorized through my dialogues with other female and male clients. They demonstrate the ways in which the everyday encounters act as important spaces/practices that inform broader understandings of the ideal and the dangerous security contractors. Such encounters, and the way we make sense of them, are articulated through the gendered encounters between the client and the contractor.

It is within broader political economic landscapes that the value of security is further defined through these everyday encounters. Just as feminists have cautioned us, the point is to read these classifications not as fixed or universal but as the product of racial, gendered, spatial, and temporal logics that produce particular seemingly fixed hierarchies of contractors. These articulations of security contractors and loose typologies should not be read as the result of the 'authentic ground truth', nor should they be read as derived from 'high' theory. Instead, these articulations are the result of re-articulations of security through everyday encounters with the men who were contracted or otherwise to protect me.

The final section, 'Bringing the researcher into the gendered critique', discusses how postionality of the research matters in the types of research one can produce. The researcher, like the subjects she researches, is gendered and her encounters are always mediated through not only how she imagines herself and performs, but also how she is interpreted by those she engages with in the field.

Producing the martial Gurkha and the flawed westerner through everyday encounters

During both my visits to Afghanistan I was protected by the very men I sought to research. Neither I, nor the clients I conversed with, had hired these men directly but we were the *end users* of their services. As was common practice, security contractors and the people they were employed to protect lived and worked in the same compounds. They often shared the same kitchens/diners, gyms, and social places. In my case, during my first visit I lived in a compound that was leased by a security company, and on my second visit I lived and worked in a compound leased by a construction company, where my neighbours were all security contractors and where their in-house security manager was in charge of our safety.

This meant that in my everyday life of running on the treadmill, preparing my meals, and commuting back and forth from cafes and restaurants or the local market I was surrounded by security contractors. These were men with, in my experience, British military training, and who had substantive commercial security experience working in Iraq and now Afghanistan. They were labelled by the industry and through self-identification as western security contractors. They continue to be the archetype contractors in popular culture, mainstream academia, and gendered accounts of security (Chisholm 2016). They are described in contradictory ways as professional and highly skilled but also as gun-obsessed and hypermasculine profiteers.

My own understandings of these contractors are ambivalent and rooted in a negotiation between what the industry and broader policy tells me about these men's ability to protect me and through everyday encounters with them as men. The industry tells us that their professionalism, rooted in their whiteness (Chisholm 2016) and their acquired military skills, makes them ideal security contractors. Yet everyday encounters, at times and as this article illustrates, can tell a different narrative. I knew them beyond their contracted security role and saw them as men who had families back home, who were often on their second or third marriages, who were cheating on their wives. I watched some stumble home drunk from a local bar, some visiting local brothels. I listened to them talk about how much they missed their families, how Afghanistan was a messed-up place, irredeemable and filled with 'oxygen-stealing corrupt men'. At the same time I saw these men confidently describe where the potential threats within the city lie, and the drills that would need to be followed to mitigate the threats and navigate the perils of the city with ease.

The white men were not the only men I encountered in my everyday life researching and being protected by security. Gurkhas – Nepalese men with collectively over 200 years of military history – with the British also protected me. However, I, like the other people detailed in this article, never knew what a Gurkha was until I went to Afghanistan. I first came across a Gurkha when I was invited to a security company Gurkha curry night. I walked into the security compound, which was a mansion, and saw the walls adorned with paintings depicting various military settings with men later confirmed to me to be Gurkhas and white British officers. The paintings displayed the Gurkhas as actively engaged in various one-on-one combat positions. They were physically smaller than their white colleagues and wore different uniforms.

I was led into a room where the curry was served and where I met many white western men working in security. Curiously, no Gurkhas were to be found. When I asked who these men were, I was regaled with numerous military anecdotes and vignettes detailing these men's fierceness and yet gentlemanliness and their childlike nature in the face of violence. Overall, I was told, a Gurkha's value comes through the management of white westerners who can harness their natural martial attributes.

Evaluating security in the professional white men and the Martial Gurkha

Gurkhas were abundant in the security industry in Afghanistan. They worked as security guards on behalf of the UN, government embassies in the city and various international commercial companies. These men were preferred security providers because the security industry leaders could draw upon racial mythologies of Gurkha martialality to naturalize their labour in order to sell it on cheaply (Chisholm 2014a) – practices that are all too common in global political economies of domestic and sex industries (Huang and Yeoh 1998; Agathangleou, 2003) and within the broader markets globally (Peterson 2005; Nevins and Peluso 2008). Where 'the industry' was assured of their security value, established through years of colonial military service to the British Empire, the clients came to know about Gurkhas, and were assured about their value, in different ways.

Beth, a female working with a commercial construction company in Kabul, found out about their reputations through online research and talking to managers of Gurkhas. Her comfort with Gurkha security labour came through what has been called 'the Gurkha security package' (Chisholm 2014a), a package including Gurkha security protection under the supervision of white western contractors. Beth stated:

'I did not have any issues with this security. Ian [the white director] was very good. Steve [the white country manager] was also very good'.

For Beth, the assurance of their value was in the fact that white western security contractors managed Gurkhas. These white contractors' military training was familiar to her. She felt she could trust that their experiences and military drills would keep her safe. Like Beth, the others I conversed with also felt the value of security came through what you knew and what was familiar to you. For both Linda and Mike (two US nationals) the US Special Forces contractors were the most desired security contractors because both knew the training they had undergone and were familiar with these men's cultural behaviour as soldiers and as contractors. Linda, for example, details:

'I knew there were a lot of Americans, ex-Special Forces, who were on the Green Village who were coming from a military training that I was familiar and comfortable with'.

Mike also felt Gurkhas could be trusted when he realized their training was closely affiliated with British military training.

I never knew the name Gurkha. I actually searched them on Wikipedia to find out what they are all about. I got the understanding that they were highly trained, handpicked, British-trained – that there was a rigorous process in selecting Gurkhas. That made me feel secure.

Leeann only became interested in Gurkhas when she found out she was going to be protected by them when she deployed to Kabul. She stated,

> I heard about Gurkhas, I was familiar with the thought process that goes behind them and their reputation. That they don't run away from bullets, that they run into bullets, which from my own experience I found to be true.

In all three cases, these clients initially preferred the security of white contractors. They were reassured of Gurkhas' security labour because of these men's colonial relations with the British (or other western forces). Such reassurance was made intelligible in the larger industry narrative that values and projects white masculine security contractors and performativities as the most professional and ideal (Joachim and Schneiker 2012; Chisholm 2014a). Yet for some I conversed with, the association of Gurkhas to white contractors was not enough to assure them of their own safety. Linda in particular expressed concern:

> In talking with my husband and deciding where to live because I had a choice at that point. One of the driving forces was actually the fact that there were more international security people at the Green Village. I wasn't comfortable by the fact that I was going to be guarded by Gurkhas, mine was more of an idea that. I really wanted to know that we would have as many weapons around as possible should anything happen.

Linda's deciding factor in picking the place to live in Kabul was based not upon Gurkhas, but on the number of US contractors who lived and worked there. Where all the people mentioned, including myself, came to know about Gurkhas first through popular books and vignettes about these men (they never run from bullets; they are fierce and brave), we remained sceptical about their security potential.

I personally felt security came through fortified spaces, armoured equipment, and personal military competency in weapons handling and hostile environment training. Linda shared my feelings of security through equipment and professional (read: western) military training. Here, Linda explained it through race, and the inability of Gurkhas (and other global South labour) to achieve the same equipment and training standards as white westerners.

Linda:

> of course race matters. It is what I'm familiar with and what I feel comfortable with. When I think of developing nations' militaries, I'm not necessarily thinking of the most capable individuals. It's through no fault of their own. Maybe they don't have the funding, the equipment. It has nothing to do with them as individuals.

For Linda, racial embodiments of contractors and their relational value in the security market mapped onto geopolitical and military inequalities. White security (observed in western military training) was seen as the ideal because it was the best funded and could spend money on training. Other races/nationalities were held suspect due to her unfamiliarity with their training – and assumptions that it was of a poorer standard because of the global South states' lower socio-economic international indicators. In this way, Gurkhas had to prove their worth to the client as men able to protect them. This largely occurred through everyday encounters with the clients, as opposed to popular cultural writings about their martial worth.

Racializing (in)security through the everyday

Security contractors were in charge of the protection and safety of clients throughout the day and night. This required contractors to be made available for both official and personal trips the client would make outside the compound as well as ensuring perimeter security of the compound which both contractors and clients often shared. In this case, the separation of work and personal life was blurred. During the official work times/in spaces that required protection in vehicles or in risk assessments and mitigation strategies, white westerners were valued for their military professional background – backgrounds familiar to those interviewed and to me. However, this was not necessarily the case during personal times and spaces involving shopping, going to the gym, and socializing. Throughout my conversations with women in particular, western contractors were often seen as a source of insecurity – one where their flirty, misogynistic jokes and male gaze made women feel uncomfortable. Alternatively, then, many women appeared to prefer the caring and distant security Gurkhas provided. Here the conversation with Beth is telling:

> We all live together in the same house and we get to know them personally whereas the Gurkhas you don't get to know them in the same way. The circumstances are different. The access I have to these 'risk managers' is different. They live in the house, they control a lot of the things we do. We eat with them, we travel with them but they refer to us as client. So I guess we see them as people like us. Maybe there is something more exotic about the Gurkhas surrounding them that we want to keep them, you see this sort of aura this person has and don't want to put a chink in that armour.

> You want that illusion or aura to be strong. You don't want to know that they are just as human as we are. I quite liked that differentiation between the Gurkha and myself because it allowed me to have this presentation in my mind of who was providing my security. Whereas now, the guys who are providing my security are just ordinary people. They make mistakes, they get scared, they get angry. But there was an aura about the Gurkhas and there is just a magic about them and maybe that's why I felt safe. They knew nothing about me but that they were contracted to protect me. It was quite special really but I don't know how much of that was in my mind ... I put my faith in these guys and hope that it never gets tested.

> Amanda: Yes, security is based upon a lot of faith.
> Beth: The other thing is too you can tell who is protecting the Americans and British and ... just from how they acted, what they were wearing ... whether it is the tight t-shirts, the muscles showing. You know I never saw a Gurkha go to the gym. You know there is this thing about the younger ones.

> Amanda: Vanity?

> Beth: Vanity and arrogance and if you are not their client they don't want anything to do with you. You don't exist. We have two projects here and one time I was in the car with the security contractor for another project and from a security point of view it was as if I didn't exist because I wasn't his client. I'm sure if something would have happened they would look after both of us but it was subtle that I didn't really matter.

> It's like two extremes. During off duty they are very friendly and on duty there is a lack of compassion. That would be a worry for me to have someone who could be two extremes.

> In the case of an emergency what are you going to get.

Beth's experiences resonated with me. There was something about intimacy being articulated differently depending on whom you were encountering. Encountering these white contractors in my everyday living, eating with them, drinking with them, going to the gym with them, and then being protected by them, I saw them as more than just security contractors. They were more than just men who were contractually obligated to keep me safe – they were men who cheated on their wives, who drank too much, who obsessed over their own body image. These were men who flirted with me in their 'off time', who made misogynist comments about UN and non-government organisation (NGO) women in the city, who lamented the security jobs they had to do and expressed frustration over clients not taking their expert advice seriously. Seeing these security contractors as flawed men who make mistakes, who contradict themselves, and who express their feelings openly created feelings of insecurity and opened up questions as to whether they would protect us when/if needed.

The dialogue between Beth and me highlights how familiarity, intimacy, and security collate differently between western and Gurkha encounters with white female clients. There is a geography that is important here. For Beth, Gurkhas' security value was assured because she never had the opportunity to see these men as other than security providers. As white women, both Beth and I were unable to overcome the colonial decorum that mediated our relations with Gurkhas. With the exception of a few Gurkhas, we only ever encountered them in their roles as security providers and ours as clients. Gurkhas were spatially segregated from our social lives. They ate and slept and socialized amongst each other. The times we encountered them in more intimate ways, when they drove us to various appointments, they waited patiently for us to finish so they could drive us home. There was a constant polite professionalism about them. They brought Beth cups of tea in the morning. They said good night and wished me happy dreams before I went to bed at night. These different geographies and uses of space allowed the perpetuation of a Gurkha myth – the idea that this is how these men always act/interact.

Such relations of intimacy mediated through re-imagined colonial encounters are also documented in feminist political economy literature on the global nannies and sex work, for example – whose labour we understand to be more valuable than that of others rests upon particular mythologies of race and gender (Agathangleou 2003). The relationship also says a lot about how we as clients define our own security and worth. This everyday security encounter was counterposed to our interactions with western contractors who fostered a paternal relationship whereby they used discourses of security to control our everyday.

Beth's and my experiences also highlight how mythologies of race and gender, of which bodies are more valuable than others, matter. Western security contractors' abilities to provide us with a safe and security environment were immediately given. We knew we could trust them because broader industry practices tell us this. These men are understood as professional. In everyday situations in Kabul they act confidently. This confidence, they tell us in various conversations, comes from military and police training in their respective western countries. However, it was through these same everyday encounters with them that their professionalism was put into question. For Gurkhas, the assurance in their security value was the opposite. I and the other clients I conversed with did not initially know about their abilities. It was through our encounters with them that our belief in their ability to keep us safe was solidified.

For Mike, Gurkha security value was seen in everyday ritualized security performances:

> Just watching the way in which [Gurkhas] handle themselves, I could tell they were doing their job in making sure the car was checked thoroughly before [being] granted access into the parking lot. So knowing about their background but also having that interaction with them and observing their shift change … I could tell they were in sync with each other so that if something went down they were well trained enough to have a coordinated response.

Beth's feelings of security with Gurkha contractors came through their ability to be respectful to the client, to keep a friendly distance from the client, and to blend into the immediate environment. She explains,

> I went on this trip around the country where we looked at UN programmes. Travelling up with them, I just found [Gurkhas] extremely respectful. They fitted in with Afghans. They didn't stand out and somehow they just seemed to meld in so I never felt we were conspicuous. They could have been taken for Tajiks or Uzbeks. It was just another layer of protection that was positive.
> Amanda: Like layer of protection because they blend in?
> Beth: Yes, they always carried weapons with them but they did blend in. We had these two, Tiger and Puna. They looked after Linda and I and when we came up to this trip they ended up providing hot water bottles for us. They would deliver a cup of tea in the morning. Those are the things I remember and it just made it so much personable. They were very real people and I felt they really cared. I never felt uncomfortable. I felt very well looked after.

In Mike's case, Gurkhas' value was proven in their everyday security rituals of checking vehicles and performing various security drills. Beth saw their value in their racialized bodies. For her, Gurkhas' value was not necessarily from their professional skillsets, or at least not entirely. Their worth came from their physical bodies, which allowed them to more easily blend into local populations. Such a logic was also highlighted by security directors I spoke to about the merits of Gurkhas' labour – that these men, given their physical bodies and their ability to speak local Afghan dialects allows them to integrate more easily (Chisholm 2014a).

In these two cases, contractors are gendered and racialized through different mechanisms. Western men are seen as professional during work hours but as a source of potential insecurity during social times. Their male gaze upon female clients and their flirtations towards the clients during 'off hours', alongside their expressed attitude towards women in general, tore away at their professionalism. Where western contractors' worth was immediately given, and then perhaps diluted through everyday social encounters, Gurkhas' worth comes in their biology (naturally blending in) and their caring abilities (bringing cups of tea). Such valuations of Gurkhas (re)produce an oriental imagining of these men that naturally separates them from their western contractor counterparts. As in the case of global South maids and nannies (Huang and Yeoh 1998; Agathangelou 2003), Gurkhas' worth is only understood through broader cultural reproductions and myths about Gurkhas, and other global South security labourers – myths that reinforce the labour divide between global South feminized natural security abilities and western security contractors whose worth is through *professional* acquired skill sets. Yet professionalism of white contractors is also not a given, but disrupted through their everyday gendered encounters, in particular with their female clients.

Leeann commented that she immediately trusted US contractors in particular because she knew their training through her own experiences of having family members in the US military. Alternatively, her belief in the value of Gurkha labour only came through an actual violent encounter in Kabul where her vehicle was only metres away from a detonated improvised explosive device (IED). She explains,

> I was in a vehicle 100 feet from another vehicle that Taliban exploded. What I saw during that time was just incredible. There is debris and falling body parts falling all over the place but there wasn't a moment where I saw anyone turn away and run. The Gurkhas were running right to the incident. Our vehicle was used as a shield during that time. I saw Gurkhas dragging other Gurkhas into the compound. They took care of their people and not only that they ran toward everything that happened. There wasn't a moment that they shied away.

In Leeann's account, Gurkhas' value was only achieved in their response to a violent encounter. They proved their worth when they ran towards the IED attack and not away. She went on to explain how Gurkhas rescued her colleagues from direct attack:

> These little tiny Gurkhas came and tackled [my very large and injured colleague] and dragged him inside for safety. These little guys stood in front of us and ran with us from the vehicle to the compound. I'll never ever forget that and I'll never question again the role that they play and when shit hits the fan, the guys are there and they are not going to run away from it.

Racialization of Gurkhas' bodies in Leeann's case then was also rooted in the long-standing cultural reproduction of martial raced men. The comment 'little tiny' here works to infantilize Gurkhas as much as it was to produce a curious juxtaposition between harmless and childlike on the one hand and fierce warriors on the other. This racial logic is also the very foundation that culturally reproduces Gurkhas as the beloved warrior gentlemen (Caplan 1995; Streets 2004) – men who are almost but not white contractors and whose value comes through association with white security or through actual demonstration of security (Chisholm 2014b).

The aforementioned cases demonstrate how none of the clients was immediately convinced of Gurkhas' merits and their ability to provide good security. This all came through personal interactions whereby Gurkhas' consistency, friendliness, diligence, and, in extreme cases, ability to react quickly and efficiently shone through. Gurkhas, unlike their western counterparts, had to prove their value to the western client, and yet their value continues to be understood through broader racial logics about these men – logics reproduced through popular cultural representations of them that perpetuation as almost but not white imagining. For Beth, and for me, Gurkhas' close association with other, white men who managed them gave us reassurance of our own security. This was then reinforced through the kindness and hospitality we received from them in our everyday interactions with them. For Mike, Gurkhas' worth was observed through regular and ritualized security performances. In Leeann's case, Gurkha masculine labour was proved through an actual violent encounter.

Where Gurkhas obtain their value through, initially, the martial myth about their military prowess, western men's value is already given – their position as professional and valued contractors already secure in an industry that rests upon the assumption that whiteness is the ideal (Chisholm 2016). Their privileged status is a product of the broader market that sustains western whiteness and western security training as the necessary 'skills' one must have to perform security (Chisholm 2016; Joachim and Schneiker 2015). Yet it is through everyday encounters of intimacy whereby such assumptions about the ideal white security are called into question.

These men's security reputations were only understood in relation to one another. We could trust Gurkhas because their natural martial masculinities have been refined and professionalized through years of service with the British military. Yet for some, this was not enough to feel safe. Gurkhas had to initially be proven by demonstration of security performances through regular and ritualized perimeter/vehicle checks and various other drills. Western men were almost immediately trusted, but then trust was lost if they were seen to be acting in contradiction to the professional security image they were known for.

Gurkha and western contractors' value is also articulated through temporal and spatial constitutions. No one interviewed ever socialized with Gurkhas the same way they did with western contractors. With the exception of a few in my own fieldwork, Gurkha men were only known through their contractual obligations to protect their clients. Consequently, because the security professional relationship was never challenged by seeing these men in any other way other than as security protection, the myth about their unfettered loyalty and professionalism was never challenged.

These types of security contractors, of course, are not universalized and are heavily dependent on context. In my own experiences and through interviews, the hypermasculine contractor was one who relied upon overt security props, tight tops, dark wraparound sunglasses and an overt showing of weaponry. Such performativities of security were detailed by Scahill (2007), embodied in the Blackwater US contractor who was concerned more about how he looked than the security he was tasked to perform. Higate (2012) also mentions the hypermasculine US contractor – referred to as the 'billy bollocks' in security training programmes.

However, for the US national clients I spoke with, they felt reassurance in these same props. James commented:

> The Americans were contractors who were personal security detail (PSD) guys. Those were the same guys for people around. Those were the same guys that would be in my same social circle and there were a difference [sic] between the Special Forces guys who were intelligent and more interesting than the 19-year-old American soldier. These guys were much more worldly. If something went down I would totally trust these American Special Forces guys. I saw them as intelligent competent people – not guys getting drunk at the bar.

For both James and Linda, the US contractor is not inherently dangerous. They see these contractors as continuing on with the ethics and professionalism they learned in the military and taking them with them into the market. Their own understandings of these men and in turn their own security works to highlight the ambiguities in these tensions between state and market. It also demonstrates how racial logics about security value and who embodies the 'right' security contractor also inform perceptions of insecurity. Implicitly trusting US contractors but requiring Gurkhas to prove their worth as security providers demonstrates this point.

Linda and James's understanding of the US Special Forces contractor offers an alternative to Higate's (2012) empirical work of hypermasculine depictions of US contractors in training programmes. Such contradictions highlight how the nationality of (and therefore familiarity with) particular military practices and appropriate masculine performativities matter in how the individual sees and reinforce gender hierarchies. For James and Leeann, because of their personal knowledge of US military training, the former US Special Forces member, now security contractor, represented the highest level of feelings of security because of his former training and his individual intelligence that originated from the professional military training he received.

Alternatively, where assurance of western value was embedded in broader understandings of the political economies of western militaries, which afforded them a high level of military training, the value of Gurkhas was rooted in their racial bodies – the naturalizing myths of who they were as men. As in Agathangelou's (2003) research on the global sex industry, it was the broader mythologies of race and gender that mapped onto the bodies of western men as highly skilled and professional and those of Gurkhas as natural warriors which provided a rationale as to why one labour force was to be instantly trusted over the other.

Gurkhas' raced bodies were rendered exotic through popular culture and vignettes that sought to naturalize them as mythical warriors. The reimagined colonial relationship that informed the everyday interactions between the clients and these men only reinforced the exotic polite gentlemen and fierce warrior mythology recounted in numerous oral and written stories about Gurkhas (Caplan 1995; Streets 2004). While their ability to keep us safe in our professional capacity, travelling to and from work for example, had to be demonstrated, for me, Linda, and Beth, Gurkhas were less likely to be a source of insecurity, through flirting and male gazes, within our personal and everyday spaces of eating, working out, and socializing.

Bringing the researcher into the gendered critique

My own trust in Gurkhas as security providers came both through me being protected by them and through my interviews with them. In both cases, I developed deep compassion for them. I watched them perform their perimeter checks of the compound I was staying in, and vehicle checks when visitors came into the compound. They stood to attention and walked with confidence. Similar to Beth's experiences, they expressed compassion towards me in their everyday mannerisms of asking about my day, and being polite but distant. They did not complain about the long hours they had to work in order to drive me to and from meetings. These men always treated me with kindness. I never felt like I was being flirted with, or that I was an inconvenience in the different errands they had to escort me on.

Through interviews I understood them as men who were deeply committed to their families, who were frustrated at times with their work conditions but never took those frustrations out on me. My encounters with Gurkhas were always underpinned by a professional protector/protected relationship founded through compassion and empathy. Their everyday encounters of asking me how I was, smiling politely, opening vehicle doors, and waving goodbye and hello as I came and went from the compound made me feel like I was not an object to be gazed upon. I saw these men with empathy as well as acknowledgment of my own privilege. Being in their presence and constantly being referred to as ma'am, while they smiled, I realized that for most, I would never form a friendship bond beyond the contractual/racialized relationship we had. They reminded me of my own privilege as a white female, filled with many entitlements they could only wish to achieve. Many men, during interviews with me, reminded me of my whiteness not only in the title they gave me, but in the polite distance they showed – in their gestures of calling me Joanna Lumley, a white female actress known for her 'saving' Gurkhas' rights to settle in the UK.

By bringing the client as a gendered (feminized) subject into the analysis, and drawing upon autoethnography methodologies, this article furthers the existing analysis on how micropractices shape gendered relations in the industry by turning the gaze to the gendered researchers. While it is no longer controversial to state our gendered bodies and performances are in part shaped by the encounters we have with those we research, spend time with, and ask questions of, this claim is rarely carried into analysis by those who research gender and war from the field. Such an epistemological stand-point opens up important analytical questions for us as researchers that include: Do the masculinities these contractors project make us feel safe? How do we negotiate control over our own bodies and space in a gendered contractual relationship where we are relegated to the protected? How do we account for these everyday encounters in our broader analysis?

Beyond the need to position the researcher in the research process, locating the everyday in how constitutions of good security are expressed demonstrates how such practices are shaping and shaped by broader articulations of security and culture capital investments in this men and masculinities are deemed important. At times the hegemonic conceptualization of masculinities was deemed a source of insecurity for those being protected; at times the marginal martial masculinities were more valued.

While my regular encounters with these men gave me important access to observe and engage in the everyday gendered security performances, and how they impacted upon me, it also was a dangerous intellectual project. How did I maintain the ability to be critical about my own complicities in my interviewees' responses in order to maintain my feminist curiosity, and in order to ask the important questions about miltiarization and how it shapes the ways in which we evaluate security, what constitutes good and bad security, and how we learn to know this? The answer is, I did not navigate this well. In many ways I was seduced by the miltiarization of security and in fact relied upon the myth of good security that was wrapped up in racial and gendered language and performances. It was not until I left this environment, after many months, that I was able to reflect upon my own complicity in the broader racial and gender processes of masculinities, security, and the private market.

For me, autoethnography is an ideal method to reflect upon my time in the field. It showcases the ways in which my emotional investment in needing to feel safe mapped onto gendered and racial embodiments of private security contractors. It demonstrates how everyday encounters with various contractors bring to the fore a multitude of masculinities that remain situated, relational, and fluid – they at times extend beyond the immediate body of the contractor. It also shows how over time and in different contexts, perceptions of 'good' and 'bad' security contracting change. While it is impossible for me to change how I behaved in the field and the logics that I relied upon for my own physical and mental well-being, this method allows me to uncover and articulate why I performed the way I did and how militarization seduced me. Such a method also calls into question the importance of all feminists researching military and security industry reflecting upon the ways their own emotional and intellectual investments might also reinforce intellectual divisions that sustain privileging particular men and masculine performativities.

That is, through capturing the researcher's own intellectual and emotional investment in the topics being researched, and the questions she finds interesting, the audience is also able to understand the processes that got the researcher to her conclusions. Such a method then potentially increases the transparency in research. It also has the ability to reveal the ways in which feminists can be (and often are) seduced by, and complicit in, reproducing the militarization logics and language of militaries and militarized masculinities.

I was seduced by the security language of the men I was being protected by; I felt like they were my friends, and I empathized with their logics, their understandings of how the world worked and what it meant to be secure. Whilst in the field, I bought into the security logics that framed my own (in)security because, for the most part, I felt safe doing so. This was made more apparent to me once I left Afghanistan and at times cringed upon rereading my own field notes. Reflecting upon my own journal entries and conversations with other clients being protected enabled me to reflect upon how the protected, in which I include myself, are a part of reproducing value associated to white racialized masculinities. Like those of others I interviewed, my perspectives of *white as best* security changed over time in the field.

By focusing on the everyday encounters between clients and contractors we begin to see how masculinities and (in)security are intimately entangled, fluid, and ambiguous. We also see how these clients, myself included, are actively reproducing imaginings of whiteness and feminization of global South labour. Western professionalism in almost all cases was assumed to be the ideal security. This was only questioned during everyday encounters of misogyny or other unbecoming behaviour of contractors during 'off time'. Gurkhas, alternatively, had to prove their value to us. This was done by their association with white managers, through their feminized labour of monotonous hours and care work (in my own and Beth's case), or through actual violent encounters (in Leeann's case). We judged their value differently. We rationalized that because their military training was not to the same standard as western contractors that they were incapable of providing the same security. We understood Gurkhas as oriental martial men whose value came through their physical bodies and their natural skills as carers and as martial warriors (when given the circumstances). Given the socio-political parameters that enabled polite but distant everyday encounters with Gurkhas, this myth of their racialized bodies was never brought into question. We did not socialize with them the same way we did with western men. Overall, these encounters suggest that imaginings of white and Gurkha security labour as seemingly naturally separated are conditioned through broader political economies of security and empire whereby we are informed what security contactors we need to value and what skills we need to look for.

Throughout my time in the field I learned valuable lessons about the ambiguities of race and how they continue to matter in shaping the ideal security provider. These ambiguities and contradictions are reproduced not only through PMSC websites and marketing campaigns and from contractors themselves, but also through the clients who consume such practices. As the different interview excerpts and my own reflections highlight, these gendered performativities are contested and negotiated. They suggest that race and gender are continually being remade, and how the marginal men and masculinities in market evaluation can often be the preferred masculine performances among the clients.

Conclusion

This article begins with the everyday as a theoretical site in order to account for how we theorize about militarism, masculinities, and war. Drawing upon the client/contractor security relationship through autoethnography, this article considers the emotional and intellectual investments that go into evaluating our own security and how racial and gendered logics filter through such evaluations. By showing the ways in which security value comes through the racial and gendered encounters between the client and contractor, this article brings to the fore the ways in which the everyday is constitutive of security value in the broader private security industry. It shows us how military masculinities are reshaped in a market-driven military economies whereby white men are not always the ideal source of security, but can also be a source of insecurity – that security value is very much contextual and geographical. In particular, conversations with those being protected have highlighted how the everyday encounters with security contractors within private and public spaces and temporalities matter in how contractors can be a source of both security and insecurity. Beth's and my own experiences in particular highlight how the white western male gazes and flirting during private social time produced discomfort and anxiety for us. Consequently, hegemonic masculinities as articulated within traditional military spaces, when brought to the market, do not always maintain the same privileged space as the archetype for security.

By focusing on the security encounters between clients and contractors and highlighting the experiences of the client, we can better understand how the industry knowledge production of whose voice counts and who are legitimate companies/ security providers extends beyond the state-market assemblages to the client on the ground. We can also begin to understand how gender embodiments of the researcher matter in knowledge production. Using autoethnographic methods also shows that my own understandings of the industry cannot be divorced from my intimate encounters with these contractors I researched. Here theories of security and gender are always embodied. As such, we need to account for the ways the ground truths of the field, of the hyper- and hegemonic masculinities, are made sense of and shaped through our experiences in the field as researchers and otherwise. Such inquires allow us to continue to conduct audits on ourselves as feminist researchers and the ways in which our work can co-opt and further advance militarism and masculinities within global politics.

Acknowledgements

I want to thank Saskia Stachowitsch, Matt Davies, Joanna Tidy, the editors of *Critical Military Studies*, and the peer reviewers for their important intellectual guidance and support in developing this article.

Disclosure statement

No potential conflict of interest was reported by the author.

ORCID

Amanda Chisholm ⓘ http://orcid.org/0000-0001-9008-2529

References

Agathangelou, A.M. 2003. *The global political economy of sex: Desire, violence and insecurity in Mediterranean nation states*. New York: Palgrave MacMillian.

Agathangelou, A.M., and L.H.M. Ling 2009. *Transforming world politics: From empire to multiple worlds*. Oxon: Routledge.

Anderson, L. 2006. Analytic autoethnography. *Journal of Contemporary Ethnography* 35, no. 4: 373–95. doi:10.1177/0891241605280449

Baker, C., V. Basham, S. Bulmer, H. Gray, and A. Hyde 2016. Encounters with the military: Towards a feminist ethics of critique. *International Feminist Journal of Politics* 18, no. 1: 140–54. doi:10.1080/14616742.2015.1106102

Barker, I.V. 2009. (Re)producing American soldiers in an age of empire. *Politics & Gender* 5: 211–35. doi:10.1017/S1743923X09000166

Butler, J. 1990. *Gender trouble: Feminism and subversion of identity*. New York: Routledge.

Butler, J. 1993. *Bodies that matter: On discursive limits of sex*. New York: Routledge.

Caplan, L. 1995. *Warrior gentlemen: 'Gurkhas' in the western imagination*. Providence: Berghahn Books.

Chisholm, A. 2014a. The silenced and indispensable: Gurkhas in private military security companies. *International Feminist Journal of Politics* 16, no. 1: 26–47. doi:10.1080/14616742.2013.781441

Chisholm, A. 2014b. Marketing the Gurkha security package: Colonial histories and neoliberal economies of private security. *Security Dialogue* 45, no. 4: 349–72. doi:10.1177/0967010614535832

Chisholm, A. 2015. From warriors of empire to martial contractors: Reimagining Gurkhas in private security. In *Gender and private security in global politics*, ed. M. Eichler, 95–113. Oxford: Oxford University Press.

Chisholm, A. 2016. Ethnography in conflict zones: The perils of researching private security contractors. In *The Routledge research companion to military research methods*, eds. A.J. Williams, N.K. Jenkins, M.F. Rech, and R. Woodward. 138–52. London: Routledge.

Chisholm, A., and S. Stachowitsch 2016. Everyday matters in global private security supply chains: A feminist global political economy perspective on Gurkhas in private security. *Globalizations* 13, no. 6: 815–29. doi:10.1080/14747731.2016.1155796

Cohn, C. 1987. Sex and death in the rational world of defense intellectuals. *Signs: Journal of Women in Culture and Society* 12, no. 4: 687–718. doi:10.1086/494362

Collins, P.H. 2009. *Black Feminist Thought: Knowledge, consciousness, and the politics of empowerment*. 3rd New York: Routledge.

Dauphinee, E. 2013a. Writing as hope: Reflections on the politics of exile. *Security Dialogue* 44, no. 4: 347–61. doi:10.1177/0967010613492838

Dauphinee, E. 2013b. *The politics of exile.* London: Routledge.

Davies, M. 2006. Everyday life in the global political economy. In *International political economy and poststructural politics,* ed. M. de Goede, 219–37. Basingstoke: Palgrave Macmillan.

Davies, M. 2016. Everyday life as critique: Revisiting the everyday in IPE with Henri Lefebvre and postcolonialism. *International Political Sociology* 10: 22–38. doi:10.1093/ips/olv006

Eichler, M. 2013. Gender and the privatization of security: Neoliberal transformation of the militarized gender order. *Critical Studies on Security* 1, no. 3: 311–25. doi:10.1080/21624887.2013.848107

Eichler, M. 2014. Citizenship and the contracting out of military work: From national conscription to globalized recruitment. *Citizenship Studies* 18, no. 6–7: 600–14. doi:10.1080/13621025.2013.865904

Elias, J., and A. Roberts 2016. Feminist global political economies of the everyday: From bananas to bingo. *Globalizations* 13, no. 6: 787–800. doi:10.1080/14747731.2016.1155797

Enloe, C. 2000. *Maneuvers: The international politics of militarizing women's lives.* Berkeley: University of California Press.

Enloe, C. 2010. The risks of scholarly militarization: A feminist analysis. *Perspectives on Politics* 8, no. 4: 1107–11. doi:10.1017/S1537592710003233

Enloe, C. 2011. The mundane matters. *International Political Sociology* 5, no. 4: 447–50. doi:10.1111/ips.2011.5.issue-4

Gray, H. 2016. Researching from the spaces in between? the politics of accountability in studying the British military. *Critical Military Studies* 2: 70–83. doi:10.1080/23337486.2016.1127554

Griffin, R.A. 2012. I AM an angry black woman: Black feminist autoethnography, voice and resistance. *Women's Studies in Communication* 35: 138–57. doi:10.1080/07491409.2012.724524

Gunaratnam, Y. 2003. *Researching race and ethnicity: Methods, knowledge and power.* London: Sage.

Henry, M. 2015. Parades, parties and pests: Contradictions of everyday life in peacekeeping economies. *Journal of Intervention and State Building* 9, no. 3: 1–19.

Higate, P. 2012. 'Cowboys and Professionals': The politics of identity work in the private and military security company. *Millennium - Journal of International Studies* 40, no. 2: 321–41. doi:10.1177/0305829811425752

Higate, P., and M. Henry 2010. Space, performance and everyday security in the peacekeeping context. *International Peacekeeping* 17, no. 1: 32–48. doi:10.1080/13533311003589165

Huang, S., and B.S.A. Yeoh. 1998. Maids and Ma'ams in Singapore: Constructing gender and nationality in transnationalization of paid domestic work. *Geography Research Forum* 18: 21–48.

Joachim, J., and A. Schneiker 2012. Of 'True Professionals' and 'Ethical Hero Warriors': A gender discourse analysis of private military and security companies. *Security Dialogue* 43, no. 6: 495–512. doi:10.1177/0967010612463488

Joachim, J., and A. Schneiker 2015. The license to exploit: PMSCs, masculinities and third country nationals. In *Gender and Private Security in Global Politics,* ed. M. Eichler, 114–30. Oxford: Oxford University Press.

Myrttinen, H. 2004. 'Pack Your Heat and Work the Streets': Weapons and the active construction of violent masculinities. *Women and Language* 27, no. 2: 29–34.

Nevins, J., and N.L. Peluso, eds. 2008. *Taking Southeast Asia to market: Commodities, nature and people in the neoliberal age.* Berkeley: Cornell University Press.

Peterson, S.V. 2005. How (the Meaning of) gender matters in political economy. *New Political Economy* 10, no. 4: 499–521. doi:10.1080/13563460500344468

Pettman J.J. 2003. International sex and service. In *Globalisations: Theory and Practice,* eds.E. Kofman and G. Young's, 157–173. London: Continuum.

Richter-Montpetit, M. 2016. Militarized masculinities, women torturers and the limits of gender analysis at Abu Ghraib. In *Researching war: Feminist methods, ethics and politics,* ed. A. Wibben, 92–116. London: Routledge.

Scahill, J. 2007. *Blackwater: The rise of the world's most powerful army.* London: Serpent's Tail.

Shepherd, L. 2008. *Gender, violence and insecurity.* London: Zed Books.

Stachowitsch, S. 2013. Military privatization and the Remasculinization of the state: Making the link between the outsourcing of military security and gendered state transformations. *International Relations* 27, no. 1: 74–94. doi:10.1177/0047117812470574

Stachowitsch, S. 2014. ʿThe reconstruction of masculinities in global politics: Gendering Strategies in the field of private security. *Men and Masculinities*, 18, no. 3: 363–386.

Stachowitsch, S. 2015. Military privatization as a gendered process: A case for integrating feminist international relations and feminist state theories. In *Gender and private security in global politics*, ed. M. Eichler, 19–36. New York: Oxford University Press.

Streets, H. 2004. *Martial races: The military, race and masculinity in British imperial culture, 1857-1914.* Manchester: Manchester University Press.

Sylvester, C. 1994. Feminist theory and international relations. In *International theory: Positivism and beyond*, eds. S. Smith, K. Booth, and M. Zalewiski. Cambridge: Cambridge University Press.

Taber, N. 2005. Learning how to be a woman in the Canadian forces/unlearning it through feminism: An autoethnography of my learning journey. *Studies in Continuing Education* 27, no. 3: 289–301. doi:10.1080/01580370500376630

Tickner, A. 2003. Seeing IR differently: Notes from the third world. *Millennium Journal of International Studies* 32, no. 2: 295–324. doi:10.1177/03058298030320020301

Tidy, J. 2015. Gender, dissenting subjectivity and the contemporary military peace movement in *Body of War. International Feminist Journal of Politics* 17, no. 3: 454–72. doi:10.1080/14616742.2014.967128

Tidy, J. 2016. The gender politics of 'Ground Truth' in the military dissent movement: The power and limits of authenticity claims regarding war. *International Political Sociology* 10: 99–114. doi:10.1093/ips/olw003

Wadley, J. 2010. Gendering the state: Performativity and protection in international security. In *Gender and international security: Feminist perspectives*, ed. L. Sojberg, 38–58. Oxon: Routledge.

Ware, V. 2016. Biting the bullet: My time with the British Army. In *The routledge research companion to military research methods*, eds. A.J. Williams, N.K. Jenkins, M.F. Rech, and R. Woodward, 231–42. London: Routledge.

Combat as a moving target: masculinities, the heroic soldier myth, and normative martial violence

Katharine M. Millar and Joanna Tidy

ABSTRACT

This article problematizes the conceptualization and use of 'combat' within critical scholarship on masculinities, militaries, and war. We trace, firstly, how combat appears as an empirical category within traditional war studies scholarship, describing an ostensibly self-evident physical practice. We then examine how feminist and gender approaches – in contrast – reveal 'combat' as a normative imagination of martial violence. This imagination of violence is key to the constitution of the masculine ideal, and normalization of military force, through the heroic soldier myth. We argue, however, that despite this critical impulse, much of feminist and gender analysis exhibits conceptual 'slippage': combat is still often treated as a 'common-sense' empirical category – a thing that 'is' – in masculinities theorizing. This treatment of gendered-imaginary-as-empirics imports a set of normative investments that limit the extent to which the heroic soldier myth, and the political work that it undertakes, can be deconstructed. As a consequence, whilst we know how masculinities are constituted in relation to 'combat', we lack the corollary understanding of how masculinities constitute combat, and how the resulting imagination sustains military authority and the broader social acceptance of war. We argue that unpacking these dynamics and addressing this lacuna is key to the articulation of a meaningfully 'critical' gender and military studies.

Introduction

In this article we explore the conceptual and normative work that 'combat' does within literature on gender and war, in particular within that grounded in theorizations of military/ized masculinities. In both academic literature and lay parlance, combat variously describes a common-sense empirical reality ('as if it were obvious and fixed, just plain combat' – Enloe 2013, 261) or a normative imagination of a very particular form of martial violence. This normative imagination underpins the masculinity-defining mythologized figure of the heroic soldier, in whom resides the 'ideals, fantasies, and desires' (Connell and Messerschmidt 2005, 838) associated with privileged iterations of masculinity.[1] This mythologized figure, in turn, is a significant locus for the political project of sustaining

44

martial authority and instating the broader social acceptance of war. Connecting an apparently objective physical practice of violence with larger issues of normative masculinity, normative civil–military relations, and legitimate state violence, the somewhat slippery conceptualization of combat grounds nearly all analyses of gender, war, and the military. What we identify as the concept's comparative under-theorization, (de)politicization, and 'common-sense' status is both puzzling and, from the perspective of a critical military/masculinities studies aimed at problematizing collective violence, in need of analytical redress.

We locate the combat-as-empirical-reality usage as most typical of traditions that include strategic studies, traditional war studies, and military sociology (hereafter 'conventional literatures'). We then discuss how the second usage, combat-as-normative-imaginary, has been developed in feminist and gender approaches to the study of masculinities, militaries, and war. In her piece 'Combat and "combat": a feminist reflection', Enloe (2013, 260) reminds us that 'combat', called upon to carry 'a burden of gendered meaning', is 'worthy of careful feminist analysis'. We argue that the unpacking of combat as a normative category has been key to the critical agenda of making visible otherwise obscured power relations through the denaturalization of that which appears 'common sense' and 'given'. This has been an important tool in deconstructing the myth of the heroic soldier, revealing and critiquing the political work that this figure undertakes.

We argue that there has, however, been conceptual slippage within critical feminist and gender approaches to the study of masculinities, militaries, and war. Combat is still called upon as a 'common-sense', or as Enloe calls it, 'obvious' (2013, 261) shorthand when describing fighting and martial violence. In other words, combat remains an empirical 'thing' across both the conventional and critical literatures – and thus becomes entangled, as a foundational 'objective' premise, with the very imaginary critical scholars seek to denaturalize and deconstruct. This limits the extent to which the heroic (combat) soldier myth, and the political work that it undertakes, may be effectively critiqued. One of the key consequences, we argue, is that whilst critical scholars have effectively grappled with the ways in which masculinities are constituted in relation to combat, we have yet to tackle, in a sustained and systematic fashion, the issue of how masculinities constitute 'combat' (as a normative imaginary). We have perhaps yet to begin even posing what is, admittedly, a counter-intuitive question. If we are to adequately illuminate the reproduction of military authority and the broader social acceptance of war, however, this critical analysis of the *co*-constitutive arrangement of 'combat' and 'masculinity' is essential. This missing piece of the puzzle allows us to better understand how martial violence is called into meaningfulness as legitimate and celebrated 'combat' along gendered lines.

The article thus proceeds by first outlining the development of combat as, initially, a theoretical concept within classical theories of war, followed by its transformation into an empirical descriptive category within modern military sociology and strategic studies. This is followed by a discussion of the animation and political interrogation of the relationship between combat and heroic masculinity in critical gender and feminist analyses. Here, we highlight, as mentioned, an inadvertent slippage between examining combat as a normative imaginary and deploying combat as an empirical category upon which to found critique. Each section provides an overview of key theoretical moves and analytic themes within two broad literatures: so-called 'conventional' military and strategic studies and 'critical' gender and feminist assessments of the military and masculinity. Both literatures, it should be noted, demonstrate Anglo-European centrism. Empirically, they consider primarily, though not exclusively, war, military organizations, and gender within the modern West and, ideologically, to a greater or lesser degree, do so from a liberal perspective. There are therefore also strong colonial and racial dimensions to the constitution of combat that, though largely bracketed here, also require substantial future analysis.

There is no bright line between the two broad scholastic churches examined here, and it is not our intention to claim that all works or all scholars falling into these traditions demonstrate the conceptual conflation of combat we problematize here. It is, instead, our aim to highlight the ways in which this conceptual slippage may occur, drawing on key exemplary texts, and the implications of this move for the broader critical project (articulated by what is otherwise frequently excellent work). To that end, the article goes on to outline the logic of the oscillation between combat-as-empirics and combat-as-imaginary by revisiting two key pieces of critical research into military masculinities: Frank J. Barrett's pioneering (1996) study of gendered/ing hierarchies within the US Navy, and Cara Daggett's innovative (2015) analysis of the queering of drone warfare. We conclude with a reflection upon the stakes of our analysis and fruitful avenues of inquiry going forward.

Combat as an empirical category

The 'commonsensical' empirical construction of combat as the basic unit of warfare is, at least in its current form, traceable to Clausewitz, and is a logically recurrent theme in modern strategic and military scholarship. For Clausewitz, fighting is the central and defining activity of the military; it is the means of achieving the ultimate (political) ends of warfare (Howard 2002, 37–8; Clausewitz 1976, 95, 142–3). Clausewitz refers to this form of fighting as *das Gefecht*, which Howard suggests ought to be translated as 'combat', referring to both a general practice (physical fighting) and a limited, temporally specific engagement (Howard 2002, 37–8). It should be noted, following Howard, that this analytical prioritization of the violent activities of the military distinguished Clausewitz from his contemporaries (Howard 2002, 37; Clausewitz 1976, 95). The fact that to many readers this equation of warfare with combat with the purpose of the military will seem obvious is a reflection of the naturalization of this formula. In other words, Clausewitz theorized and constructed combat, and its relationship to modern warfare, as a concept, rather than the empirical description of the true, or factual, nature of warfare it is often taken as today. As *On War* became canonized as the seminal work on modern warfare (Howard and Paret 1976, viii–ix) – indeed, the nature of war itself – the subtle theoretical aspect of Clausewitz's work was occluded.

The layered conceptualization of combat as 'obviously' physical fighting, the building-block of warfare, and the primary activity of the military, strongly informed – as empirical premise – the subsequent development of nineteenth- and twentieth-century understandings of war and the military (Strachan 2012; see also Nordin and Oberg 2015, 394).[2] In the twentieth-century post-war era, military sociologist Morris Janowitz argued that although the majority of military personnel, resources, and activities are no longer directly involved in combat, 'military authority...must strive to make combat units its organizational prototype' (1959, 480). For

Janowitz, these combat units are 'functionally distinguished' (480, fn10) from other aspects of the military by their engagement in dangerous, physical 'battle' (481) – or combat as a practice of fighting. Janowitz' contemporary, Samuel Huntington, similarly reiterated Clausewitz's understanding of combat as the physical practice of war – armed, between individuals or groups of individuals, and violent (1957, 11). Like Janowitz and Clausewitz, Huntington regards the balance of the military organization as relevant only insofar as it supports the military's central mandate: combat (1957, 11–12).

This naturalization of Clausewitz's theoretical conceptualization of combat (and its relationship to the broader military enterprise) into a descriptive, 'found' empirical category, is still more apparent in the term's usage throughout the contemporary strategic studies literature. Posen, for instance, in his analysis of the modern mass army, refers to its 'combat power' – the ability of the military to effectively conduct organized violence (1993, 84). Colin Gray reflects a similar understanding of combat in his study of 'national style' in military strategy, arguing that US officers in WorldWar II were trained to be logistically ready for combat, while German officers were trained in the practice of combat – fighting between conventional military groups (1981, 25–6). This synonymity of combat with 'simply' war fighting is perhaps best reflected in Stephen Biddle's work, which, arguing for the continuing relevance of land war and conventional arms, refers to 'old-fashioned close combat against surviving, actively resisting opponents' (2003; see also Betts 1994, 2016).

This is not to say that this literature lacks normative discussion. The vast majority of classical theories of war, strategic studies, and, particularly, military sociology, are concerned with the appropriate regulation and political (civilian) control of military violence (see Millar 2016). Huntington, for instance, is clear that it is this mandate for fighting that separates the military from the civilian sphere (1957, 11). Like Clausewitz, Huntington is keen to provide the institutional and political context – the state-sanctioned military – that distinguishes combat, as legitimate violence, from other forms of interpersonal physical confrontation. Janowitz, interestingly, goes further, unproblematically referring to the credibility of combat 'heroes' as an objective factor in military authority and organization, rather than a subjective judgment (1959, 479). The normativity of this discussion, however, is displaced from the conceptualization of combat itself, which is static, to the relationship between combat and military and civil authority. Combat may enable individuals to distinguish themselves, or be put to positive or negative political ends, but is not a normative category or practice in and of itself – it simply 'is'.

This correspondingly apoliticized understanding of combat is most evident in the large literature regarding combat motivation. Shils and Janowitz's early study of the Wehrmacht in WWII laid the groundwork for this decontextualization by not only reproducing an understanding of combat as 'stubborn fighting', but also by emphasizing the irrelevance of broader political concerns to individual motivation and combat efficacy (1948). Dave Grossman, in his controversial finding of soldiers' apparent reluctance to kill, propounds a similarly circumscribed understanding of combat as direct killing in a military context, and 'combat veterans' as those who were present in the physical space of battle (1996). More recent studies of combat cohesion, though arriving at different 'diagnoses' of combat motivation (e.g. group solidarity vs. training and drill), maintain a similar framing of the problem, and thus underlying conceptualization of combat: Given that combat is violent and dangerous, and contravenes civilians' social norms, why fight? (see, for instance, King 2015; Wong et al. 2006; Newsome 2003). Throughout, though a distinction is occasionally drawn between close, physically proximate (infantry) combat and contemporary missions flown by fighter pilots (see Grossman 1996, 234; Robben 2006), the conventional strategic and military sociology literature produces a common, purportedly empirical description of combat. It is constructed as a discrete, physical event, and as therefore possessing a definitive '"before" and an "after"' (Bourke 2000, 11). It is also, as implied by Clausewitz's emphasis upon *fighting*, spatially limited in scope, as war *per se* involves a variety of practices beyond a physical engagement. Though technology and political context may change, combat is also, by implication, a sufficiently uniform practice and experience of physical fighting that, as an empirical category, it may be applied across diverse conflicts.

Mainstream approaches to military and strategic studies are also alive to the relevance of gender (or, in many cases, more accurately, sex) to combat. It is understood to be the practice of men, as both an historical regularity (see Best 1998, 31; Goldstein 2001; Van Creveld 2000) and a 'proving' or 'testing' ground for masculinity (see, for instance, Stouffer et al. 1949; Van Creveld 2000). Early studies on the relationship between masculinity and combat articulated the notion that it was a given and findable empirical phenomenon. In their study of military socialization, Arkin and Dobrovsky (1978, 156; see also Eisenhart 1975) note, for instance, 'that it is in combat that the core of masculinity is demonstrated', through showing 'courage, [and] lack of squeamishness' (Stouffer et al. 1949, quoted in Arkin and Dobrovsky 1978, 156). They detail how combat capacity and experience stratify the military institution both formally and informally, privileging and elevating those assigned to and experiencing combat.

This constitution of combat (and war) as the sole preserve of men is not posited as an active matter of conceptual construction, but rather as empirical description. Combat is a 'thing' against which masculinity might be tested and through which it might be demonstrated, but it remains very much a fixed empirical reality. Generally, though not uniformly, as a result of both historical production and ontological approach, this literature represents sex/gender, and thus men and masculinity, as correspondent. Consequently, the male/masculine (as interchangeable) nature of combat is apoliticized and naturalized into the empirical description of an objective social phenomenon. That said, in these emphases on the 'fraternal order' of the military (Janowitz 1959) – and centrality of masculine solidarity to combat motivation – normative characteristics subtly begin to creep into the ostensibly descriptive empirical label. This is perhaps most evident in the polemical literature arguing for women's exclusion from combat, exemplified by Martin Van Creveld (2000). The conventional military/strategic literature, despite its inclinations towards positivist social science, is not immune to conceptual 'slippage'. This is something feminist scholarship has given much more attention to, as we consider below.

Durieux provides a cogent summary of the conventional literature's understanding of combat as, 'on the individual level, [a practice] in which a soldier gives death to another and exposes himself to the deadly blows of his adversary' (2012, 143). As illustrated by this brief review, combat, as an empirical category, refers to violent, plausibly reciprocal activity, involving elements of both killing and risk, between men. Though the literature exhibits a normative preference for the regulation of this fighting under the auspices of the military, and by the state, the empirical practice of combat itself is supposedly removed from issues of politics (and, potentially, ethics). This apoliticization of combat via empiricism – not entirely in keeping with Clausewitz's explicitly theoretical conceptualization – and its connection to men/masculinity have been problematized, as we explore next, by a robust feminist, masculinities, and critical military/militarization research programme. Within this work, however, vestiges of the empirical status/existence of combat have survived. As indicated by critical engagement with the 'heroic soldier myth', empirical combat as masculine activity often forms a jumping-off point for gendered analysis, rather than an object of deconstruction in its own right.

Combat as normative category

In contrast to the approaches reviewed above, the aim of critical feminist and gender approaches to the study of the military and war is not to problem-solve issues of military power, but rather to problematize this power (Basham, Belkin, and Gifkins 2015, 1). Though far from monolithic, this 'critical' approach can be characterized by its sceptical curiosity, 'questioning underlying assumptions, investigating things that conventional commentators typically leave unexplored' (Enloe 2015, 3). It can also be said to 'approach...military power as a question rather than taking it for granted' (Basham, Belkin, and Gifkins 2015, 1). A key component of this project is making visible the gendered power operating in war, the military, and the international system, and, ultimately, 'how *much* power it takes to maintain the international political system in its present form' (Enloe 1989, 3, emphasis is original). These interventions reveal that there is nothing inevitable or natural about the configurations of international politics in and through which we all live; it is not satisfactory to say of any aspect of these political orderings 'it's just the way it is'. This tradition of scholarship is sceptical, therefore, of 'common sense'.

Correspondingly, feminist and gender approaches articulate a suspicion of the ostensibly descriptive, 'simply' empirical account of the military and combat provided above. In particular, critical approaches question the unproblematic bundling of sex/gender into 'soldier' that underlies empirical combat, as well as the explicit bracketing of normative concerns regarding the legitimacy of state violence (see Dawson 1994, 1). In contrast, feminist and gender approaches have, in effect, conceptualized combat as a normative category that carries a heavy 'burden of gendered meaning' (Enloe 2013, 260). Combat, in other words, as a concept, is not correspondingly reflective of an actually existing and obvious practice, but rather encapsulates a range of assumptions concerning socially valued masculinity, civil–military relations, violence, physical geographies, and the state.

Megan Mackenzie, for instance, in her detailed examination of socio-cultural myths regarding the long-standing (though now defunct) US military policy of excluding women from combat, observed that 'the definition of combat itself is elusive: both "combat" and "combat exclusion" are constructed' (2015, 19). In sharp contrast to the conventional literature, which accepts the definition of combat as stable and objective, Mackenzie highlights the historical contingency of the concept as changing over time, in accordance with the military's needs (32–3; see also Enloe 2007, 82). Similarly, Zalewski observes a disconnect between the empirical fact that 'relatively few men who have been in the military have ever been in combat' and the hierarchical valorization and prioritization of 'combat' by the military institution, as seen in the conventional writings above (1995, 353). Zalewski suggests that this construction is furthered by the 'ideological potency' of combat, which, though having no fixed definition, is 'wielded as a criterion to separate the "men from boys"' and, of course, women from men (353). Unpacking combat as a normative category, therefore, involves interrogating the conditions of its social construction and the politics it contains and obscures (Enloe 2013).

Key to this project, as implied by the illustrative quotations above, is an examination of the relationship between combat and normative idealizations of socially valorized masculinity, as articulated within the context of the military. As has been well established in the literature, for critical scholars, there is no singular (or self-evident) 'military masculinity'. Masculinities are not static, monolithic sets of character traits or types (Connell 1995; and see Duncanson 2009, 64), nor do they correspond to essentialist constructions of sex. Instead, just as 'militaries… are not unified or homogenous structures' (Sasson-Levy 2003, 320), there are a 'multiplicity' of (military) masculinities (Kirby and Henry 2012, 445; Barrett 1996; Baaz and Stern 2009, 499) within and across institutions. Understood as 'values, capacities, and practices' (Hutchings 2008, 402), military masculinities and the idealized 'selves' they conjure are models rather than tangible realities (Woodward 2000, 644; see also Duncanson 2009, 65). Together, these masculinities – and femininities (Sjoberg 2007; Stachowitsch 2013, 161) – reflect and reproduce hierarchical orders of gender, race, and class (Messerschmidt 2012, 73).

Combat is identified by critical scholars as central to the articulation of these hierarchies, and their reproduction outside the formal institution. Not entirely unlike the military sociologists above, critical scholars observe that the institutions of war and the military function as 'a crucial arena for the construction of masculinity in the larger society' (Hale 2012, 700; Connell 1995). Rather than acting as a 'proving ground' for an *actually (pre)existing* maleness, however, the military (re)produces a '(variable) set of values, capacities, and practices that are identified as exemplary for men' (Hutchings 2008, 402; Connell and Messerschmidt 2005, 832), or as Belkin puts it (2012, 3) a 'set of beliefs, practices and attributes' that are widely valued and privileged within society.

More specifically, critical scholars argue that it is through the idea of combat that these beliefs and practices are articulated. Combat, they observe, is constituted within the military as a particular imagined space of idealized violence in which soldiers can 'prove their manhood' (Enloe 2013, 260). Combat masculinity is therefore characterized within the literature as typified by stereotypically masculine, socially valorized attributes, such as 'aggressiveness and endurance of hardships and physical toughness' (Hale 2012, 705; see also Connell 1995), risk-taking, discipline, technological mastery, absence of emotion, and rational calculation (Barrett 1996, 140). Within the constellation of military masculinities, critical work frequently refers to 'the hegemonic masculinity of the combat soldier' (Sasson-Levy 2003, 327), as both additional military and civilian masculinities are (implicitly or explicitly) articulated in reference to this idea. Both conventional and critical literatures are therefore concerned with the relationship between men and the military – particularly in the crucible of combat. They differ substantially, however, in ontology. For conventional scholars, 'real men' pre-exist combat, and prove their mettle within it. From the critical perspective, the military, through its institutional emphasis on the priority of combat, produces 'real men', reifies the notion that there is such a thing as 'real men', and promulgates authoritative ideals of masculinity.

Coupled with this contingent, though socially ordering, understanding of masculinity, combat becomes a normative imaginary of martial violence through which gendered ideals, fantasies, and desires can be organized.[3] The exact form of that imagination might change or be contingent to a particular process of masculinity formation, but it remains an 'anchor' for the social (re)production of military masculinities (Hale 2012, 713; Duncanson 2009, 65; Woodward 2000). Various configurations of the notions of risk (Barrett 1996), proximate killing (Daggett 2015, 365), and reciprocity of violence (Enloe 2013, 260) define combat as a gendering category. As a special, celebrated, and exclusive domain of violence and of gender definition and meaning, combat 'is contested, protected, and negotiated' (Enloe 2013, 261). It is imagined in various ways to define who is 'in' and 'out' of particular privileged categories. Being associated with combat, critical scholars observe, accords privileges (Tidy 2016).

In this sense, combat is understood by the critical literature to constitute a point of positive linking and negative differentiation (Duncanson 2009, 67–8, following Hansen 2006). The apparent monopoly over combat (and therefore hegemonic masculinity) sets the military apart from other parts of society; it is the fundamental point of differentiation through which the military can be imagined as apart and special, occupying the privileged side of the (also imagined) civil–military divide. The difference between this claim and the similar one made by writers such as Clausewitz and Huntington hinges on whether combat is seen as a 'real' thing, empirically differentiated from other forms of interpersonal violence, or a socially produced and embedded category of gender and power. As discussed further below, combat therefore performs an immense amount of analytical work in the critical deconstruction of the military: it is posited as a constructed, empirical 'site' wherein military personnel enact and negotiate their gendered/ing social identity and institutional status, and, more problematically, as a conceptual anchor for the analysis of the hierarchies these negotiations produce.

Combat and the heroic soldier myth

The critical leverage proffered by this treatment of combat as a gendered normative imaginary is perhaps best illustrated by gender and feminist theorists' empirical identification, and subsequent critical deconstruction, of a cultural figure crucial to the normalization – and depoliticization – of combat: heroic (combat) soldiers. In doing so, critical scholars are able to foreground the normative assumptions (and political commitments) smuggled into the ostensibly objective observations of the conventional literature. The conventional writers discussed at the outset, though to varying degrees of explicit acknowledgment, propound and rely upon the idea of the heroic soldier. Dave Grossman's 'Introduction' to the revised (2014) issue of his *On Killing* offers, for example, a straightforward statement of his normative position. The book, Grossman writes:

> is being read by countless thousands of warriors who are called upon by our nation to kill in combat. And it is the single greatest honor of my life to have been of service to these magnificent men and women....

Grossman neatly encapsulates the interrelation of combat, nation, and some form of elevation or glory (in his formulation it is 'magnificence') attributed to soldiers. Feminist scholars add gender to this nexus, and deconstruct it as a site of gendered power rather than a 'common-sense' 'good'.

As Sasson-Levy (2003, 327) notes, it is 'almost impossible to constitute a military identity (masculine or feminine) that does not relate to the identity of the warrior' or as Duncanson (2009, 64) describes it, the 'warrior model'. The existence of multiple masculinities (and femininities) in a military context, as noted above, should not distract from the structures of power asymmetry which they entail: 'the hegemony of the warrior model is part of the reason that certain men dominate within the military, [and] why there is pressure on men to conform to this form of masculinity (Duncanson 2009, 65). The military is a space within which 'gender' – and other axes of power and subordination – are made, learned, practised, and reproduced (see Baaz and Stern 2009, 499) and combat is a crucial conceptual anchor point for this gendering and all that it entails both in military training and during war. As Duncanson (2009, 65) describes, '[m]any accounts of military training demonstrate how gender informs this process, as all things "feminine" are disparaged, and "manhood" is equated with toughness under fire' (although cf. Belkin 2012).

Within this literature, the myth of the magnificent warrior is grounded in a heroic narrative of combat, an imagination of martial violence that is privileged, powerful, and strongly normative. The heroic soldier myth may change (see Dawson 1994; Cooper and Hurcombe 2009, 103), but it remains persistent (Woodward, Winter, and Jenkings 2009, 219), largely due to the grounding provided by combat in the soldier's relationship with the polity. As combat is imagined to involve elements of risk, sacrifice, and violence on behalf of the group (Mackenzie 2015, 34), the hierarchical elevation of the soldier over the civilian population is assured, despite changes in the 'actual' empirical practice of martial violence over time. Within feminist and gender analysis, combat as a normative category therefore remains relationally stable, though substantively changeable. As the heroic (combat) soldier 'expands our own ego boundary ecstatically into that of the nation' (Butler 2006, 145), warfare is therefore understood through the figure of the soldier (Woodward, Winter, and Jenkings 2009, 219; Woodward and Jenkings 2012, 351). The 'legitimacy or otherwise' (Woodward, Winter, and Jenkings 2009, 211) of war, and the overall political community, is thus affirmed or contested (see for example Achter 2010; Tidy 2016; Millar 2016) through the lens of this figure.

Significantly, the combat imaginary that produces the 'heroic soldier' parallels, at an individual level, state–state combat, such that the heroic soldier is imagined as a microcosm of the heroic state. The heroic soldier, foundationally constituted by combat, is therefore presented as an ideal of, simultaneously, masculinity and citizenship (Sasson-Levy 2002). As Dahl Christensen identifies, '[t]he soldier becomes a proponent for a whole society's set of values' (Dahl Christensen 2015, 355). Deconstructing the myth of the heroic soldier – and its constitutive relationship between combat and masculinity – is therefore key to the critical project of feminist and gender scholarship. If it seems to be common sense that soldiers are heroic, that they do a thing called combat, and that this combat is in some ways an elevated and special form of violence, then it is the job of critical scholars to unpack the assumptions, and trace the political investments and the power relations that do powerful work both 'out there', in military discourse and popular imaginary, and 'in here', in our own scholarship.

Combat as an (un)moving target

As the above overview has demonstrated, understanding combat as a normative imaginary reveals the gendering, highly 'powered' 'work' that it does. The specific content of combat is contingent and flexible, and it is called upon and into being in particular forms at particular times to associate, disassociate, include, and exclude from particular, privileged categories of military masculinity and their 'attendant promises and entitlements' (Baaz and Stern 2009, 499). Unpacking combat as a normative imagination, or model, of martial violence has been a means of bringing to the surface the constitution of privileged forms of gender and the power relations that are entailed. It has revealed the constructed and *deconstructable* form of the mythical heroic soldier, and 'his' role in instating and normalizing gendered, martial power and its associated state violence. This has been key to the critical knowledge project of feminist and gender approaches.

As we will now argue, however, this same literature demonstrates a tendency towards 'slippage' between the two ways of using the notion of combat. To put it bluntly, combat becomes 'plain combat' (Enloe 2013, 261), including in work that also deconstructs it as a normative imagination, submerging and smuggling its normative heritages and investments into scholarly work that is otherwise concerned with the critical knowledge project. This can hamper analysis of the complexities of the 'burden of gendered meaning' that 'combat' carries (Enloe 2013, 260), and risks reproducing the gendered and gendering asymmetries entailed in it.

In some instances within the literature on military/ized masculinities, the importance of combat to the constitution of masculinities is noted in a broader and almost obligatory sense, but then the analysis 'moves on' without tracing precisely what is meant by combat in the particular setting being examined, or unpacking what gendering 'work' it is doing there (Barrett 1996; Duncanson 2009). Higate (2003), for instance, in the major 2003 edited volume *Military Masculinities*, questions whether 'the presence of some women, particularly at the heart of the male bastion of face-to-face combat, is likely to affect the nature of the combat masculine warrior ethic?' (205). Here, though Higate explicitly identifies combat as masculine and problematizes essentialist views of women as 'importing' femininity into the military, he also reiterates the male nature of physical, reciprocal combat – combat as obvious practice – and its apparent centrality to military identity. It is correspondingly unclear whether Higate is referring to combat as masculinist normative imaginary, employing its construction within the military itself, or is himself analytically deploying an empirical understanding.

Similarly, the critical literature, particularly when working to highlight the elision of marginalized persons – and masculine/feminine subjectivities – within both the military institution and broader citizenship myths, frequently relies on an empirical conceptualization of combat. This is something exemplified in our own previous work. In her examination of the public representation of deceased US female soldiers, for instance, Millar refers to the awkwardness of the contrast between US official combat exclusion policy and 'actual combat practice' (2015, 766; see also Holland 2006, 3; King 2015, 122–3) – employing an empirical understanding of combat to, in essence, censure the US military for misrepresenting the experiences of women. A similar slippage is evident in Tidy's (2016) discussion of the privileging of combat experiences within the public discourse of the military dissent movement and the broader gendered asymmetry of war knowledge. Whilst Tidy argues that the focus on combat soldiers reproduces a narrow conceptualization of war, marginalizing the experiences of large portions of the military, her discussion of the political power of 'experiences of combat' (100) tacitly maintains combat as an empirical 'thing' (see also Perez and Sasson-Levy 2015).

In other instances, combat is used as an empirical descriptor, perhaps by referring to a 'combat soldier' or a 'non-combat soldier' (Sasson-Levy 2003, 2008; Woodward 2000; Tidy 2016) or referring to soldiers having seen or been in combat (Stachowitsch 2013; Daggett 2015; Duncanson 2009). In doing so, the literature slides between conceptual references to the figurative heroic soldier, a potentially useful conceptual construct, and seemingly habitual references to 'actual' soldiers engaged in a real practice. Our cited examples here are not meant to be exhaustive. As indicated by our citation of many these same writers in our discussion above, the work we critique has been crucial to theorizing military/ized masculinities and unpacking combat as a normative category. We argue that the criticality of this collective work could be enhanced, however, through a conceptual attention to combat that avoids slippage between empirical and normative category.

In sum, the critical literature slides towards the reification of combat as empirically real, in a vein that largely duplicates the constructions of the conventional literature upon which its critique is built, and in doing so also reifies a particular normative relationship between combat and masculinity. Christensen and Jensen, in their (2014) critique of the hegemonic masculinities literature, observe that patriarchal power relations – men's domination over women – have been definitionally incorporated into the key concept of 'hegemonic masculinity' (64). Christensen and Jensen suggest that although patriarchal power relations may characterize the great majority, if not all, of empirically observed hegemonic masculinities, importing this empirical regularity as a necessary conceptual assumption limits the critical power and insights of the resulting scholarship (64). As argued by Beasley, 'it is politically deterministic and defeatist to assume that the most dominant...ideals/forms of masculinity are necessarily the same as those that guarantee authority over women' (2008, 88, in Christensen and Jensen 2014). The conceptual assumption of men's dominance over women undermines, in other words, the potential power and emancipatory potential of critical gender work by premising its central critique upon the existence of the relationship it seeks to problematize and replace.

The implicit reliance upon an empirically real combat, as key to producing not just masculinity, but *the* central, militarily and socially valorized masculinity (the heroic soldier), encounters a parallel structural problem. If, as outlined above, the central problematic of the critical feminist/masculinities/military research agenda is the deconstruction of the gendered relationships and associations that produce the political possibility/ies for violence and/or war, the conceptual importation of an apparent empirical relationship between masculinity and combat undercuts its analytic and political potential. In other words, it is difficult to critique, deconstruct, and constitute alternatives to the heroic soldier myth premised upon the 'proving ground' of combat when this precise relationship is 'baked into' the empirical/normative slippage of the concept itself.

The treatment of normative-combat-as-empirical is a specific, arguably foundational, iteration of a general problem Hutchings (2008) outlines as characterizing the gender and war literature. Hutchings observes that in instances wherein masculinity is constructed as 'materially necessary to war because of what war is taken for granted to be…war anchors masculinity, in the sense that the meaning of masculinity reflects the requirements of war' (Hutchings 2008, 393). This dynamic is redoubled, and specified, by the conceptual ambiguity of combat, wherein what Hutchings refers to as the 'causal, or conditional' argument relating war to gender, described above, is rolled into a single concept, as an assumption. This empiricization removes and obscures the argumentative and directional aspect of this relationship – that combat produces the heroic, hegemonically masculine, soldier. The critical literature thus correspondingly risks (re) producing the essentialized understanding of combat/gender of the conventional literature, wherein combat is inherently masculine, and hegemonic masculinity will, inevitably, refer to, or be positioned against, combat violence. Similar to men, as observed by Morgan, 'seeking the best of reasons to distance themselves from dominant and harmful models of masculinity', so too may critical scholars 'unwittingly perpetuate a one-dimensional and quasi-naturalistic model of "man the warrior"' (1994, 179).

Unlike the broader gender and war literature, which holds space for examining the ways in which 'masculinity anchors war, in the sense that it provides a framework through which war may be recognised, understood, and judged' (Hutchings 2008, 393), we currently lack a corresponding critical awareness of, and attention to, the role of gender in constituting combat. As a result, we are unable to interrogate combat as a gendered (and classed, racialized, sexualized) structural category, social identity, and process – as *political*. We have only a partial grasp of a complex process of mutual constitution.

Implications of 'slippage': revisiting key texts with view to co-constitution

By way of closing, we demonstrate in detail the process of conceptual slippage and its implications for critical analysis by revisiting two influential studies of combat, the military, and masculinity that we cite as both significant to the theorization of military masculinities, including combat as a normative category, and illustrative of the broader problem of slippage we identify. In doing so, we re-read these texts' empirics from the perspective of the *co-constitution* of gender and combat to provide an initial demonstration of the critical pay-off of our argument. We begin with Barrett's (1996) study of masculinities in the US Navy. We then discuss Daggett's (2015) discussion of US military masculinities, drones, and the queering of killing in war. We have chosen these pieces because they represent, in Barrett's case, an influential early theorization of the topic that has been widely cited, and, in Daggett's case, a strong piece of contemporary theorizing on military masculinities. Both pieces successfully theorize military masculinities as a hierarchically organized plurality rather than a monolith, and illuminate the inter-relation of combat, manliness, and soldierliness. Whilst Daggett's analysis undertakes this more explicitly than Barrett's, both pieces can be read as concerning the maintenance of the heroic soldier myth and the production of martial violence as 'combat'. Both pieces, however, illustrate the conceptual slippage that we described above which limits the extent to which these inter-relating dynamics can be critically unpacked.

Frank Barrett's article represents an approach to combat and masculinities that owes much to the more conventional, empirical usage we discussed above. However, the gender-normative character of the notion is more fully realized here than in those literatures. Within the broad canon of military masculinities research, the article was particularly valuable in how it deconstructed what had elsewhere been characterized as a more monolithic military masculinity, revealing varying 'constructions of masculinity…across [Navy] job specialties' (Barrett 1996, 129). Barrett set out to complicate 'the link between masculinity, violence, and the military' captured in the common-sense 'image of "man the warrior"' (Barrett 1996, 130).

Throughout the analysis, combat appears as an anchor of military masculinity, and central to the pursuance of the heroic ideal. Gender is defined in relation to combat, which remains an empirical 'thing' around which gendered identities orientate. In Barrett's analysis, the relational ranking of masculinities in the US Navy places the 'combat speciality' of aviation at the top, and the 'combat speciality' of surface warfare second, with 'non-combat' 'support communities' (131) occupying 'the lowest status in the Navy' (138). Those working in support communities 'have [in contrast to their combat-specialist colleagues] fewer opportunities to demonstrate courage, autonomy, and perseverance, the hallmark of the hegemonic ideal' (138). Barrett therefore highlights how combat is an organizing feature of the gender structure of the US Navy. In this analysis, however, combat remains a common-sense 'thing' that some encounter and some don't, rather than a particular hegemonic imaginary of martial violence. The piece reveals the ways in which the heroic soldier myth is maintained, by privileging those that have the most direct contact with violence and disparaging those who are further from it – a gendered proximity–distance configuration which Daggett (2015) develops in her work.

Conceptualized as an empirical thing – albeit strongly normative – combat can define gender but does not seem to be in turn defined by it. This means the work that gender does to privilege and legitimize violence cannot be fully traced. Close reading of the piece hints, however, at the ways in which combat is, rather than a static and straightforward opportunity to demonstrate particular ideals, a normative imagination not only constituting but also constituted by gender. Barrett notes that naval aviators, those with the highest status, are understood within the institution as 'embodying the ideal' of masculinity (134). This is associated with involvement in 'combat' but also 'boldness, irreverence' and 'aggressive heterosexual activity' (134). Barrett records that 'for those [pilots] who engaged in combat, the experiences were unforgettable'; 'the most intense experiences of their lives' (134), expressed as 'feelings of transcendence and vitality' that are 'usually reserved for the sacred' (135). These accounts can be re-read as examples of how very particular imaginaries of violence call moments of warfare into meaning in particular, *valued and privileged* ways. In the case of one of Barrett's interviewees, a pilot, particular tropes of the combat imaginary (proximity, death, reciprocal danger) are mapped onto the account of flying 'the entire length and breadth of Kuwait in one day' so that it can become intelligible as 'flying combat in the

Gulf'. There is death, for example – 'the burned out tanks, the bodies' – and there is some form of reciprocal peril: 'if you hit a telephone wire you were dead'. Proximity is emphasized; the aviator describes flying '10 feet above the ground' (Barrett 1996, 135). The 'coding' of flying as combat is a function of gender working at the broadest level of framing. The attachment of the figure of the masculinity-embodying aviator to flying enables flying to be understood as 'combat', and in order to be intelligible in these terms risk, reciprocity, and proximity are emphasized. The construction of this warfare as combat within the terms of the heroic myth works, therefore, to simultaneously maintain the heroic myth *and* 'code' this particular violence as glorious, right, and legitimate – or even bordering on sacred.

In Frank Barrett's study, combat is treated as an empirical given, albeit one with a strongly normative, gender-defining, and gendered-power-organizing association. In Cara Daggett's (2015) exploration of drone warfare, to which we next turn, we see combat appear as both normative and empirical category, with the distinction or relation between the two not always clearly apparent. Combat is here understood as a synonym for 'killing in war', and as a normative form of martial violence that must be (re)imagined, protected, and sustained.

Daggett unpacks how drones make the categories of martial violence 'strange', troubling the 'common sense' of its privileged and fetishized forms. The co-constitution of combat and masculinity are submerged but present dynamics in the analysis. Daggett notes that martial violence is 'located along the hierarchy of militarized masculinities that helps to render killing in war morally intelligible' (2015, 362) and at the same time the 'orienting "straight" path of killing in war' constitutes 'a compass for militarized masculinities' (363). She describes how this '"straight" path of combat [provides]…familiar landmarks (enemy, courage, combat, coward)' that offer 'moral and practical bearings for killing in war' (362). In this way, combat is clearly at work as a normative imaginary, locating the soldier hero and the good wars 'he' fights and co-constitutively locating violence as morally intelligible or not through a mapping of that violence onto the 'hierarchy of militarized masculinities' (362). These '"lines" that orient state violence' and are 'a compass for militarized masculinities' are 'queered' by drones (363); drones pose a problem for the straightforward operation of the soldier myth. 'The pinnacle of hegemonic warrior masculinity' is located 'at the site of intimate killing in the midst of combat, with other experiences judged by their proximity to this point'. As with Barrett's Gulf War pilot, emphasizing reciprocity, danger, and proximity, 'hegemonic warrior masculinity is secured not just through the difficult act of killing up close, but in doing this while making one's body vulnerable to being killed' (365). Yet, 'because drone operators are protected from death, they are disqualified from performing as "real" warriors because their bodies are not sited in combat' (363).

The normative work that the combat imaginary undertakes is therefore a key part of the analysis. A sense of gender and combat as mutually constituting comes through. Yet combat is at the same time regularly deployed as a synonym for 'killing in war'. It is noted that an 'increasing share of combat [is] performed by drone assemblages' (369) although 'Drones have not completely replaced more traditional combat' (375). 'Drone warfare make[s] combat on homesites while at the same time these agents of violence avoid entering idealized sites of combat' (366). Empirical combat-as-killing is therefore subdivided into that which is 'idealized' (and therefore normative) and that which is not; it might have varying normative rank but in the final analysis it remains an empirical thing that just 'is'. As with Barrett's analysis, there remains something 'common sense' about this conceptualization of combat that shifts it out of the ambit of analysis and critique because it appears given rather than constitutable. It remains 'offstage'; a thing against which masculinities and other forms of martial violence can be measured. The *constitution of the measure* remains obscured.

Because a common sense of combat-as-killing-in-war is retained, the politics of producing this martial violence *as combat* (or the failure to do so) cannot be fully brought into focus. Daggett notes that drone violence 'cannot be located along traditional gendered maps that orient killing in war' (364), to which we think it is important to add *as combat* (or not). Drone operators make visible the instability of the heroic soldier myth, which must be preserved and protected. But they also make visible the instability of legitimate martial violence. There is little to qualitatively separate the violence of a missile fired from a drone from that fired from a naval aviator's F18. These acts of martial violence can be 'coded' very differently, however, within imaginaries of gender and violence, so that one is straightforwardly understood as combat (as in Barrett's study) and one is not (as Daggett describes). As is apparent from Daggett's empirical source material, the public discrediting, mocking, and broader feminizing of drone pilots who have claimed that they are engaged in combat (369) is achieved by highlighting how they might rupture the myth of the heroic soldier. Doing so is at the 'cost' of placing drone killings in an ambiguous ethical space: they are not fully counted as valued and privileged, good and righteous combat. Drone operators are termed the 'chair force' and they are commonly represented sitting in 'ergonomic chairs, drinking coffee and eating junk food' (367), the only danger posed by an accidental burn from a hot pocket (368).

If we understand masculinity as constituting combat,[4] we should pay attention to the ways that imaginaries of violence, embedded in the heroic soldier myth, call moments of martial violence into value and legitimacy. If we do so, drone killings arguably pose more of a problem to the straight lines orienting gender and war than is accounted for in Daggett's analysis, because they pose a problem for the category of combat itself. To return to Barrett's Gulf War pilots, the line between one-sided martial violence being combat or not might come down to how easily the respective dangers of phone lines and hot pockets can be accommodated within a maintenance regime for the heroic soldier myth. In this way, the maintenance of the heroic soldier myth and the myth of legitimate martial violence are co-constitutive projects. Drones, at least for now, destabilize combat itself, the common-sense basic unit of warfare.

Conclusion

Scholarship does not exist externally to public narratives of soldiers, soldiering, violence, and war. Deconstructing the figure of the soldier is key to the intervention that critical feminist and gender work undertakes in this context, and the concept of military/ized masculinities has been a useful tool for achieving this. In this paper we have aimed to take seriously the point that there is nothing 'obvious' (Enloe 2013, 261) about combat. Writing within the critical feminist tradition we have felt uneasy, including with our own work, at the ways that a well-rehearsed link between masculinities and combat can slip into a tacit common sense that combat is a 'thing'. Does this common sense hamper us in our efforts to deconstruct militarist myths such as that of the heroic soldier, and, further, might it represent a continuing investment in that myth?

A 'common-sense' empirical conceptualization of combat characterizes the conventional literatures on war that feminist and gender approaches have written against. But we have argued that it survives in these critical literatures. We suggest that this tenacious common sense does two related things. Firstly, it obscures the co-constitution of gender and combat as a privileged and war-legitimizing imagination of martial violence. If combat is just a 'thing', then it is easy enough to see how martial manliness can be produced through association and exposure to it, but less easy to see the extent to which ideas of martial manliness (with its entailed legitimacy) in turn produce war violence as combat. Put another way, imaginations of combat are a way for soldiers to 'prove their manhood' (Enloe 2013, 260). But how and in what ways is violence 'proved' against imaginations of manliness? How does violence become combat – and therefore a legitimate mode of martial violence – through association with particular imaginations of manhood? Gender is the engine of combat as a moving normative target. A blurred definitional treatment of combat constrains our analytic ability to reveal the co-constitution of gendered power and privileged imaginations of violence.

Secondly, the common sense of combat is a perpetuation of the investment in the idea of the heroic soldier and the legitimate wars he fights. Combat is not a straightforward synonym for violence. The word invites associations that cannot easily be dispelled; the word 'combat' is therefore never just a word – rather, it is a key term in a lexicon that perpetuates the epistemic normalization and – indeed – *celebration* of state violence. To use combat as an empirical descriptor is to invest in the legitimacy of the broad and imaginative array of violences meted out by the state. This does not, of course, mean we should avoid talking about combat. Quite the opposite: we should take claims to and about combat seriously and understand the gendered and gendering and more broadly political work that such claims undertake. We should also take seriously denials of combat; when soldiers who have been involved in martial violence deny that this violence was combat (for example see Strong et al. 2015), it is important to understand why. Ultimately, what we must not do is allow combat to be common sense, a thing that is beyond the reach of our feminist curiosity (Enloe 2004).

Notes

1. When we refer to soldiers we mean here a martial figure encompassing the different branches of the modern western military (i.e. army, navy, and air force).
2. Indeed, this understanding of 'war as fighting', albeit in a more open and contingent sense than articulated by Clausewitz, has been proposed as a key aspect of the nascent field of 'critical war studies', which otherwise departs from the assumptions of classical theories of war. See Barkawi and Brighton (2011).
3. As we will discuss later, it should also be understood as operating in the other direction: the ideals of martial masculinity organize this imagination of violence in particular ways that undertake specific political tasks.
4. And, indeed, femininity as well – though this conceptual assemblage will likely take substantial empirical work to unravel.

Acknowlgments

We thank the anonymous reviewers for their insightful comments and guidance, Victoria Basham at Critical Military Studies, and participants at the "Masculinities at the Margins: War Beyond Hypermasculinity" workshop (Newcastle University, April 22–24, 2015).

Disclosure statement

No potential conflict of interest was reported by the authors.

References

Achter, P. 2010. Unruly bodies: The rhetorical domestication of twenty-first-century veterans of war. *Quarterly Journal of Speech 96*, no. 1: 46–68. doi:10.1080/00335630903512697

Arkin, W., and L.R. Dobrofsky. 1978. Military socialization and masculinity. *Journal of Social Issues 34*, no. 1: 151–68. doi:10.1111/josi.1978.34.issue-1

Baaz, M.E., and M. Stern. 2009. Why do soldiers rape? Masculinity, violence, and sexuality in the armed forces in the Congo (DRC). *International Studies Quarterly 53*, no. 2: 495–518. doi:10.1111/isqu.2009.53.issue-2

Barkawi, T., and S. Brighton. 2011. Powers of war: Fighting, knowledge, and critique. *International Political Sociology 5*, no. 2: 126–43. doi:10.1111/ips.2011.5.issue-2

Barrett, F.J. 1996. The organizational construction of hegemonic masculinity: The case of the US Navy. *Gender, Work Organization 3*, no. 3: 129–42. doi:10.1111/gwao.1996.3.issue-3

Basham, V.M., A. Belkin, and J. Gifkins. 2015. What is critical military studies? *Critical Military Studies 1*, no. 1: 1–2. doi:10.1080/23337486.2015.1006879

Belkin, A. 2012. *Bring me men: Military masculinity and the benign façade of American empire, 1898–2001*. New York: Columbia University Press.

Best, G. 1998. *War and Society in Revolutionary Europe 1770–1870*. Guernsey: McGill-Queen's University Press.

Betts, R. 1994. The delusion of impartial intervention. *Foreign Affairs 73*, no. 6: 20–33. doi:10.2307/20046926

Betts, R. 2016. The soft underbelly of American primacy: Tactical advantages of terror. *Political Science Quarterly 131*, no. 2: 449–69. doi:10.1002/polq.v131.2

Biddle, S. 2003. Afghanistan and the future of warfare. *Foreign Policy 82*, no. 2: 31–46.

Bourke, J. 2000. *An intimate history of killing: Face-to-face killing in twentieth-century warfare*. New York: Basic Books.

Butler, B. 2006. *Precarious life: the powers of mourning and violence*. London & New York: Verso

Christensen, A.D., and S.Q. Jensen. 2014. Combining hegemonic masculinity and intersectionality. *Norma: International Journal For Masculinity Studies, 9, No. 1*: 60-75.

Clausewitz, C. 1976. *On war*. Trans. and eds. M. Howard and P. Paret. Princeton: Princeton University Press.

Connell, R.W. 1995. *Masculinities*. Cambridge: Polity Press.

Connell, R.W., and J.W. Messerschmidt. 2005. Hegemonic masculinity rethinking the concept. *Gender & Society 19*, no. 6: 829–59. doi:10.1177/0891243205278639

Cooper, N., and M. Hurcombe. 2009. Editorial: The figure of the soldier. *Journal of War & Culture Studies 2*, no. 2: 103–04. doi:10.1386/jwcs.2.2.103_2

Daggett, C. 2015. Drone disorientations: How 'unmanned' weapons queer the experience of killing in war. *International Feminist Journal of Politics 17*, no. 3: 361–79. doi:10.1080/14616742.2015.1075317

Dahl Christensen, T. 2015. The figure of the soldier: Discourses of indisputability and heroism in a new Danish commemorative practice. *Journal of War & Culture Studies 8*, no. 4: 347–63. doi:10.1179/1752628015Y.0000000026

Dawson, G. 1994. *Soldier heroes: British adventure, empire and the imagining of masculinities.* Oxon & New York: Routledge.

Duncanson, C. 2009. Forces for good? Narratives of military masculinity in peacekeeping operations. *International Feminist Journal of Politics* 11, no. 1: 63–80. doi:10.1080/14616740802567808

Durieux, B. 2012. The history of grand strategy and the conduct of Micro Wars. In *The Oxford handbook of war*, eds. J. Lindley-French and Y. Boyer, 135–45. Oxford: Oxford University Press.

Eisenhart, R.W. 1975. You can't hack it little girl: A discussion of the covert psychological agenda of modern combat training. *Journal of Social Issues* 31: 13–23. doi:10.1111/josi.1975.31.issue-4

Enloe, C. 1989. *Bananas, beaches and bases.* London: Pandora Press.

Enloe, C. 2004. *The curious feminist: Searching for women in a new age of empire.* Berkeley and Los Angeles: Univ of California Press.

Enloe, C. 2007. *Globalization and militarism: Feminists make the link.* Lanham: Rowman and Littlefield Publishers, Inc.

Enloe, C. 2013. Combat and 'combat': A feminist reflection. *Critical Studies on Security* 1, no. 2: 260–63. doi:10.1080/21624887.2013.814857

Enloe, C. 2015. The recruiter and the sceptic: A critical feminist approach to military studies. *Critical Military Studies* 1, no. 1: 3–10. doi:10.1080/23337486.2014.961746

Goldstein, J. 2001. *War and gender.* Cambridge: Cambridge University Press.

Gray, C. 1981. National style in strategy: The American example. *International Security* 6, no. 2: 21–47. doi:10.2307/2538645

Grossman, D. 1996. *On killing.* Boston: Little Brown.

Grossman, D. 2014. *On killing.* New York: Open Road Integrated Media

Hale, C. 2012. The role of practice in the development of military masculinities. *Gender, Work & Organization* 19, no. 6: 699–722. doi:10.1111/gwao.2012.19.issue-6

Hansen, L. 2006. *Security as practice.* Oxon & New York: Routledge

Higate, P. 2003. Concluding thoughts: Looking to the future. In *Military masculinities: Identity and the state*, ed. P. Higate. New York: Praeger.

Holland, S. 2006. The dangers of playing dress-up: Popular representations of Jessica Lynch and the controversy regarding women in combat. *Quarterly Journal of Speech* 92, no. 1: 27–50. doi:10.1080/00335630600687123

Howard, M. 2002. *A very short introduction to Clausewitz.* Oxford: Oxford University Press.

Howard, M., and P. Paret. 1976. Introduction in Clausewitz, C. On war, Howard, M. and P. Paret, eds and trans., Princeton: Princeton University Press: vii-xxx

Huntington, S. 1957. *The soldier and the state: The theory and practice of civil-military relations.* Cambridge, MA: Harvard University Press.

Hutchings, K. 2008. Making sense of masculinity and war. *Men and Masculinities* 10, no. 4: 389–404. doi:10.1177/1097184X07306740

Janowitz, M. 1959. Changing patterns of organizational authority: The military establishment. *Administrative Science Quarterly* 3, no. 4: 473–93. doi:10.2307/2390811

King, A., ed. 2015. *Frontline: Combat and Cohesion in the twenty-first century.* Oxford: Oxford University Press.

Kirby, P., and M. Henry. 2012. Rethinking masculinity and practices of violence in conflict settings. *International Feminist Journal of Politics* 14, no. 4: 445–49. doi:10.1080/14616742.2012.726091

Mackenzie, M. 2015. *Beyond the band of brothers: The US military and the myth that women can't fight.* Cambridge: Cambridge University Press.

Messerschmidt, J.W. 2012. Engendering gendered knowledge: Assessing the academic appropriation of hegemonic masculinity. *Men and Masculinities* 15, no. 1: 56–76. doi:10.1177/1097184X11428384

Millar, K. 2015. Death does not become her: An examination of the public construction of female American soldiers as liminal figures. *Review of International Studies* 41, no. 4: 757–79. doi:10.1017/S0260210514000424

Millar, K. 2016. Mutually implicated myths: The democratic control of the armed forces and militarism. In *Myth and narrative in international politics*, ed. B Bliesemann de Guevara, 173–91. Abingdon: Palgrave MacMillan.

Morgan, D. 1994. Theater of war: Combat, the military, and masculinity. In *Theorizing masculinities*, eds. H. Brod and M. Kaufman, 165–82. Thousand Oaks: Sage.

Newsome, B. 2003. The myth of intrinsic combat motivation. *Journal of Strategic Studies* 26, no. 4: 24–46. doi:10.1080/0141-2390312331279678

Nordin, A., and D. Oberg. 2015. Targeting the ontology of war: From Clausewitz to Baudrillard. *Millennium* 43, no. 2: 392–410. doi:10.1177/0305829814552435

Perez, M., and O. Sasson-Levy. 2015. Avoiding military service in a militaristic society: A chronicle of resistance to hegemonic masculinity. *Peace & Change* 40, no. 4: 462–88. doi:10.1111/pech.2015.40. issue-4

Posen, B. 1993. Nationalism, the mass army, and military power. *International Security* 18, no. 2: 80–124. doi:10.2307/2539098

Robben, A. 2006. Combat motivation, fear, and terror in twentieth-century argentinian warfare. *Journal of Contemporary History* 41, no. 2: 357–77. doi:10.1177/0022009406062073

Sasson-Levy, O. 2002. Constructing identities at the margins: Masculinities and citizenship in the Israeli army. *The Sociological Quarterly* 43, no. 3: 357–83. doi:10.1111/tsq.2002.43.issue-3

Sasson-Levy, O. 2003. Military, masculinity, and citizenship: Tensions and contradictions in the experience of blue-collar soldiers. *Identities, Global Studies in Culture and Power* 10, no. 3: 319–45.

Sasson-Levy, O. 2008. Individual bodies, collective state interests the case of Israeli combat soldiers. *Men and Masculinities* 10, no. 3: 296–321. doi:10.1177/1097184X06287760

Shils, E., and M. Janowitz. 1948. Cohesion and disintegration in the Wehrmacht in World War II. *The Public Opinion Quarterly* 12, no. 2: 280–315. doi:10.1086/265951

Sjoberg, L. 2007. Agency, militarized femininity and enemy others: Observations from the war in Iraq. *International Feminist Journal of Politics* 9, no. 1: 82–101. doi:10.1080/14616740601066408

Stachowitsch, S. 2013. Professional soldier, weak victim, patriotic heroine: Gender ideologies in debates on women's military integration in the US. *International Feminist Journal of Politics* 15, no. 2: 157–76. doi:10.1080/14616742.2012.699785

Stouffer, S., et al. 1949. *The American soldier. V. 2 Combat and its aftermath*. Princeton: Princeton University Press.

Strachan, H. 2012. *Strategy and war in the oxford handbook of war*, Lindley-French, J. and Y. Boyer, eds. Oxford: Oxford University Press: 30–42

Strong, J.D., P. Findley, S. McMahon, and B. Angell. 2015. What is war? Female Veterans' experiences of combat in Iraq and Afghanistan. *Affilia* 30, no. 4: 489–503. doi:10.1177/0886109915585383

Tidy, J. 2016. The gender politics of "Ground Truth" in the military dissent movement: The power and limits of authenticity claims regarding war. *International Political Sociology* 10, no. 2: 99–114. doi:10.1093/ips/olw003

Van Creveld, M. 2000. Less than we can be: Men, women and the modern military. *Journal of Strategic Studies* 23, no. 4: 1–20. doi:10.1080/01402390008437809

Wong, L., et al. 2006. *Why they fight: Combat motivation in the Iraq war*. Carlisle Army Barracks, PA: Army War College Strategic Studies Institute.

Woodward, R. 2000. Warrior heroes and little green men: Soldiers, military training, and the construction of rural masculinities. *Rural Sociology* 65, no. 4: 640–57. doi:10.1111/j.1549-0831.2000. tb00048.x

Woodward, R., and N.K. Jenkings. 2012. Military memoirs, their covers and the reproduction of public narratives of war. *Journal of War & Culture Studies* 5, no. 3: 349–69. doi:10.1386/jwcs.5.3.349_1

Woodward, R., T. Winter, and K.N. Jenkings. 2009. Heroic anxieties: The figure of the British soldier in contemporary print media. *Journal of War & Culture Studies* 2, no. 2: 211–23. doi:10.1386/jwcs.2.2.211_1

Zalewski, M. 1995. Well, what is the feminist perspective on Bosnia? *International Affairs* 71, no. 2: 339–56. doi:10.2307/2623438

Unmaking militarized masculinity: veterans and the project of military-to-civilian transition

Sarah Bulmer ⓘ and Maya Eichler

ABSTRACT

Feminist scholarship on war and militarization has typically focussed on the making of militarized masculinity. However, in this article, we shed light on the process of 'unmaking' militarized masculinity through the experiences of veterans transitioning from military to civilian life. We argue that in the twenty-first century, veterans' successful reintegration into civilian society is integral to the legitimacy of armed force in Western polities and is therefore a central concern of policymakers, third-sector service providers, and the media. But militarized masculinity is not easily unmade. Veterans often struggle with their transition to civilian life and the negotiation of military and civilian gender norms. They may have an ambivalent relationship with the state and the military. Furthermore, militarized masculinity is embodied and experienced, and has a long and contradictory afterlife in veterans themselves. Attempts to unmake militarized masculinity in the figure of the veteran challenge some of the key concepts currently employed by feminist scholars of war and militarization. In practice, embodied veteran identities refuse a totalizing conception of what militarized masculinity might be, and demonstrate the limits of efforts to exceptionalize the military, as opposed to the civilian, aspects of veteran identity. In turn, the very liminality of this 'unmaking' troubles and undoes neat categorizations of military/civilian and their implied masculine/feminine gendering. We suggest that an excessive focus on the making of militarized masculinity has limited our capacity to engage with the dynamic, co-constitutive, and contradictory processes which shape veterans' post-military lives.

Introduction

Feminist scholars have focussed on the 'making' of militarized masculinity, especially the making of a 'hypermasculinity' of soldiers so often associated with war and militarism. They have paid less attention to the ways in which militarized masculinity is expected to be *unmade* after release from the military. But examining the experiences of veterans can offer valuable opportunities to deepen our understanding of the contemporary gendering of war and militarism. In the aftermath of the wars in Iraq and

Afghanistan, the veteran has become a significant social and political figure in many Western societies.[1] Occupying the space between military and civilian life, war and peace, and the domestic and the international, veterans are key protagonists in the negotiation of relations between geopolitics, the state, the military, and society. They inhabit a privileged, typically masculine, subjectivity and are often held up as model citizens who have made sacrifices for the state, a position that they can leverage in diverse ways, to campaign for better benefits or to wage anti-war campaigns. Yet they are also marginalized and can struggle to access employment and services in support of their transition from military to civilian life. Veterans challenge societies by bringing distant foreign wars home to their national and local communities. As the complex embodied legacies of war and war-preparedness, veterans can be understood to be an 'excess' of war.

In the twenty-first century, Western policymakers and service providers, as well as the media and wider public, are paying increasing attention to the transition of military personnel back into the civilian world. The 'successful' reintegration of veterans is integral to legitimizing the deployment of armed force in contemporary liberal democracies. Yet the process of transition for veterans is not so straightforward. As we show, it involves the negotiation of masculinities and femininities across military and civilian spheres in complex, and often contradictory, ways. Veterans often have an ambivalent, and sometimes hostile, relationship with the state and the military. Simultaneously, militarized masculinity is embodied and experienced, and has a long and contradictory 'afterlife' in veterans themselves. The very liminality of 'unmaking' militarized masculinity troubles and undoes neat categorizations of military/civilian and their implied masculine/feminine gendering.

The acknowledgment that the boundaries between military and civilian worlds, and between masculinity and femininity, are porous calls into question the ability of feminists to identify what the boundaries of a militarized masculine identity *are*. This prompts us to reconsider what is at stake in drawing such conceptual boundaries in our own analyses and through our concepts, and what we might be obscuring as a result. We argue that, in the case of veterans, the focus on militarized masculinities has exceptionalized veterans' experiences by privileging their military identity at the expense of the civilian identity they are in a process of acquiring, limiting our ability to engage with the entangled, co-constitutive, and contradictory social processes which shape veterans' post-military lives. Ultimately, we argue that feminist interrogation of this process of unmaking militarized masculinity in veteran transition compels us to consider the ways that veterans' experiences may exceed feminist conceptualizations of 'militarization', challenging the coherence of the concept of militarized masculinity itself.

We begin by outlining the ways in which feminist scholarship has focused on the construction of militarized masculinities. This brief exegesis locates the horizons of feminist thinking on militarized masculinities within recent debates concerning the ontological instability of militarized masculine identities, the performative reproduction of gender power in feminist critiques, and a tendency to be deterministic around possibilities for the transformation of militarized masculinities. We then introduce elite discourses of military-to-civilian transition, demonstrating that these are a conscious attempt to manage the process of unmaking of militarized identity, a process which is complex, contradictory, and ultimately incomplete. Finally, we offer a discussion of the implications of veterans' experiences for feminist theorizing of militarized masculinity.

Making militarized masculinity in feminist scholarship

Militaries have been important sites for feminist investigations into the gendering of world politics. This work has identified a cultural ideal which associates masculinity and combat through the valorization of strength, athleticism, aggression, (hetero)sexual conquest, and brotherhood. As Enloe explained in 1988, this is because

> Militaries depend on the maintenance of a popular presumption that the most rewarded, highest status military activities can go only to the masculinized members of society ... [and they] need to keep alive the notion that, for men, having intimate relationships with the military is the best proof that they are 'real men'. (90–1)

Feminist investigations treat militarized masculinity (and sometimes 'military masculinity'[2]) as something to be explained, specifically analysing how military and masculine ideals merge in different historic and geographic contexts. The concept of militarized masculinity has been politically important to feminists because it recognizes that there are no inherent connections between masculinity and militarization, but that masculinities become militarized and therefore can potentially be demilitarized (Enloe 2000).

The empirical focus of feminist research has tended to be on the *making* of militarized masculinity, or, to put it another way, the processes through which men become militarized. The concept has been used to describe and theorize the privileging of masculinity to military organizations, documenting the discourses and practices which reproduce and reify hegemonic masculine norms within military cultures. Feminists have offered incisive analyses of the ways hegemonic ideas about masculinity are central to the recruitment, training, and deployment of soldiers (*inter alia* Enloe 2000; Goldstein 2001; Klein 2003; Whitworth 2004; Brown 2012; Eichler 2012; Basham 2013). They have argued that pervasive cultures of militarized masculinity explain resistance to the integration of women and LGBT personnel within militaries (*inter alia* Cohn 1998; Herbert 1998; Sasson-Levy 2003; Mankayi 2006; Woodward and Winter 2007; Bulmer 2013). Whilst hegemonic ideas of militarized masculinity are important, research has shown that militaries rely on many complementary, and sometimes contradictory, forms of militarized masculinity to function (e.g. the military clerk, logistics officer, medic, etc.) (Enloe 1988; Higate 2003; see also Titunik 2008; Conway 2008; Parpart and Partridge 2014). These moves have effectively diversified, pluralized, and complicated feminist understandings of militarized masculinities.

Feminists have shown that the construction of militarized masculinities, and related femininities (see for example Sjoberg and Gentry 2007), have serious consequences. Basham's (2013, 140) study of British military personnel demonstrates that the understandings of gender, race, and sexuality which structure the 'routinised, everyday ordering of bodies' within the British military are integral to the projection of violence abroad. The privileging of militarized masculinity in wider society has been identified as a key mechanism through which war and imperialism are legitimized more broadly (McClintock 1995; Tickner 2001; Cockburn 2010) and through which states gain legitimacy as the masculinized defender of the feminized nation which is embodied by women and children (Runyan 1990; Peterson 1992; Young 2003; Eichler 2012; Sjoberg 2013). Feminists have also recognized that warrior masculinity may be contested, and have been interested in uncovering the alternative and marginalized masculinities within militaries that do not conform to the ideal type of 'militarized masculinity that occupies "hegemonic space"' (Parpart and Partridge 2014, 562). They have explored the ways contestation over the meaning of militarized masculinities has been important for understanding anti-colonial struggle (Parpart 2015), conscientious objection (Conway 2012), draft evasion (Eichler 2012), and other forms of resistance.

However, recent contributions to the study of militarized masculinity have challenged some of the fundamental understandings of previous scholarship. As the role and composition of Western militaries has changed, scholars have debated whether there is potential to transform militarized masculinities. Some have argued that peacekeeper masculinities, which seemingly challenge traditional ideas about militarized masculinity, are in fact adaptive masculinities which create new gendered and racialized hierarchies (Orford 2003; Razack 2004; Whitworth 2004). Duncanson (2015) argues that this is not only pessimistic but also problematic because there is 'a tendency to overdeterminism' that cannot conceptualize 'progressive change' (240). She instead points to the emergence of a peacekeeper masculinity which incorporates feminine traits such as empathy and communication, suggesting the potential for substantive change (Duncanson 2013). Duncanson and Woodward (2016) make a similar argument in the context of women's growing participation in militaries and the need to engage with the possibility of 'regendering' the military. This work continues to focus on the construction of militarized masculinities but questions the gendered 'content' of these identities and their potential for change.

Other scholars have complicated understandings of the making of militarized masculinities by challenging the ontological coherence of the identity itself. Unlike earlier conceptualizations which suggested that militarized masculinities were constructed through oppositional hierarchical traits such as masculine/feminine and dominant/subordinate, Belkin's (2012) study of US recruits found that they were routinely compelled to engage in behaviours that are supposedly disavowed by masculinity, such as military hazing rituals involving the penetration of other men, indicating that militarized masculinity is structured by contradictions 'designed' to confuse recruits and ensure obedience. Drawing on a performative understanding of gender (Butler 1999), others have explored the ways in which militarized masculinity is haunted by its own (im)possibility (Bulmer 2013; Forthcoming 2018; Welland 2013). For example, Bulmer (2013) demonstrates the radically unstable and contingent nature of all military identities through her discussion of the integration of LGBT personnel, and the resultant confusion about their status. The implication of this mode of critique is, as Welland argues, that in continuing to analyse militarized masculinities feminists performatively reaffirm the power of gender by giving it a coherence it does not possess. Stern and Zalewski (2009, 616) call this the 'sex/gender paradox' or 'predicament', which refers to the way that feminist interventions necessarily reinvoke the 'very grammars that initially incited them as narratives of resistance' and become complicit in the violences they seek to ameliorate. These interventions encourage renewed reflection about the validity of militarized masculinity as a concept, and the *effects* of using it in feminist research.

We aim to contribute to this questioning of established, often taken-for-granted, assumptions about militarized masculinities. However, instead of focusing on the construction of militarized masculinity we focus on the possibilities for its *unmaking*. We argue that in the figure of the veteran, we can interrogate what it might mean to 'unmake' militarized masculinity, and reflect on what the implications of this are for feminist theorizing. We begin with a discussion of elite attempts to manage military-to-civilian transitions in contemporary Western states and the experiences of veterans who undergo these transitions.

Military-to-civilian transitions

State interest in veterans, and the experiences of veterans themselves, has varied historically and geographically, depending on national and social contexts. For example, after the First World War, the British and German governments treated their disabled veterans very differently. In Britain they were largely neglected by the state and reliant on philanthropy, and this was accepted by veterans' organziations, which promoted the idea of 'Service Not Self' (Cohen 2001, 3). In contrast, German veterans secured generous state support yet became increasingly politicized, blaming both the Weimar government and the public for their ingratitude (Cohen 2001). Veterans, who are often held up as model citizens, can cause political problems for state elites because their dissent can seriously compromise a government's credibility (Enloe 2011). For example, American veterans of the Vietnam War were able to mobilize significant support for their anti-war campaigns due to their role as former soldiers (Hunt 1996).

The end of the Cold War brought about a dramatic change in the tempo and scope of Western military deployments. The changing character of conflict and the emergence of 'new wars' (Kaldor 1999) was seen to reduce the willingness of Western publics to tolerate military casualties, signaling an era of 'post-heroic warfare' (Luttwak 1995; Coker 2002; Scheipers 2014). Commentators pointed to the 'virtual' and spectacular nature of modern warfare which distances Western military personnel and publics from the corporeal realities of war by the use of 'clean' or precision weapons (Baudrillard 1995; Der Derian 2001). However, after the 9/11 attacks and the subsequent wars in Afghanistan and Iraq, Western publics have once again been confronted with the embodied effects of ground campaigns as a result of a large number of military deaths and military personnel returning to their societies with life-changing injuries. These protracted military campaigns have also lacked consistent support among Western publics. As a result, there has been a concerted effort by elites in the US, the UK, and Canada to improve public perceptions of the armed forces, which has led to the emergence of a 'support the troops' discourse which aims to rhetorically distance military personnel from the wars they are fighting in (Stahl 2009; McCready 2013; Ingham 2014; Basham 2016). It is within this context that Western governments and publics have developed an awareness of a new generation of veterans.

In countries such as the US, Canada, or the UK, the transition from military to civilian life has been recognized as a key concern. Western countries are increasingly trying to support military-to-civilian transition through a suite of services and benefits delivered by military, state, third-sector, and private providers. For example, the US Department of Veteran Affairs runs a compulsory Transition Goals, Plans, Success

(Transition GPS) programme which provides 'comprehensive services to our nation's Servicemembers to transition to work, life, and home after the military'. Transition GPS includes 'individual transition planning' and a 'customized roadmap' to make transition easier (Department of Veteran Affairs 2017). In Canada, the Department of National Defence (DND) and Veterans Affairs Canada (VAC) offer vocational rehabilitation programs aimed at facilitating the transition of serving military members to civilian life. The DND programme focuses on career transition services (DND and CAF 2016), while VAC's Rehabilitation Program for ill and injured veterans includes medical, psychosocial, and/or vocational rehabilitation (VAC 2016). In the UK, the Veterans Agency is part of the Ministry of Defence (MoD) and its remit is to help 'ex-service personnel get appropriate support from government, local authorities, independent bodies and the charity sector' (Veterans UK 2017).

The purpose of the New Veterans Charter that came into effect in Canada in 2006 'is to facilitate the re-entry of veterans into civilian life in a way that promotes reintegration and independence' (Aiken and Buitenhuis 2011, 3–4). In the UK, the Armed Forces Covenant (Ministry of Defence 2011, 8, our emphasis) 'involves an obligation for life … [that] the commitment and sacrifices made by veterans in the past, as well as their *continuing value to society*, should be properly recognised in the support they receive'. Service-leavers are conceived of as an 'extraordinary resource' (Lord Ashcroft 2014, 9). For those who are injured the aim is to enable a 'smooth transition to an appropriately skilled civilian life' (Ministry of Defence 2012). This is conceptualized broadly to mean that the veteran has housing and employment, does not require special medical attention, and is independent (not dependent on welfare). As Lord Ashcroft (2014) argues, 'good transition is important for the country' because, having invested in the training of military personnel, good transition can 'ensure that those individuals are in a position to be *net contributors* to society' (7, our emphasis).

Implied in these statements is the understanding that 'bad' or failed transition will result in veterans being a burden on society, alongside other 'non-productive' individuals. This renewed focus on the management of military service-leavers in the twenty-first century reflects growing concerns about the social, political, and economic costs of 'failed' transition. A veteran is considered to have successfully transitioned when he or she has adapted to the requirements of civilian society. Sayer et al. (2011) have defined the transition as the 'achievement of satisfactory levels of functioning at home, at work, in relationships and in the community' (3). Research has focused on the increased prevalence of homelessness, substance abuse, unemployment, mental health problems, criminality, and violence among veterans (*inter alia* Iversen et al. 2005; Brown 2011; Brunger, Serrato, and Ogden 2013; van Hoorn et al. 2013; Ashcroft 2014). The economic cost of 'failed' transition is substantial; for example, it is estimated that the cost to the British state in 2012 alone was 'upwards of £113 million, and the financial cost to the charity sector and to the individual was many times more' (Forces in Mind Trust 2013, 2).

Alongside mitigating the effects of war and military service and the associated costs, it is important to recognize that some state elites now view 'successful' transition as a core component of military recruitment and retention. In the UK, *The Veterans' Transition Review* (Lord Ashcroft 2014, 29), commissioned by Prime Minister Cameron to provide a 'review of the policies currently in place regarding Service

Leavers' transition to civilian life, the provision made by the state and others, and the practical experiences of those leaving the Forces', states that:

> ensuring a good transition is more than a matter of meeting our obligations to a series of individuals. It can help to promote the core functions of our Armed Forces, and consequently should not be thought of as a fringe activity. This is because good transition can make a difference to what I term the four 'R's: Recruitment, Retention, Reputation and the Reserves. (Ashcroft 2014, 7)

The rehabilitation of injured personnel, many of whom are ultimately discharged, is also intimately connected with recruitment and morale within the armed forces. With regards to rehabilitation, the MoD recognizes that rehabilitation of service-leavers is crucial for Britain's ability to project military power. The Defence Medical Rehabilitation Centre (DMRC) at Headley Court, the UK's premiere centre for military rehabilitation, has 135 hostel rooms for 'force generation' patients and 96 in-patient beds. Force generation patients are those who attend short courses needed to return to deployable fitness. The in-patients are those most severely injured who require intensive treatment and are not expected to redeploy. For the MoD, both groups of patients are 'equally important to defence' because 'DMRC'S force generation work supports the physical component of fighting power whilst its rehabilitation of complex trauma cases supports the moral component' (MoD 2013).

Questions over veterans' benefits and services have become particularly acute in the context of austerity economics which has seen cuts to public services and welfare across the Western world. Despite the policy interest in veteran transition, the cost of support has increasingly been devolved onto the third sector. Over the past decade there has been a proliferation of charitable or non-profit organizations in the US, Canada, and UK that provide services and programmes for veterans (Mumford 2012; Herman and Yarwood 2015; Eichler 2015). Mumford (2012) has described the heavy reliance on the third sector in the provision of care to UK veterans as 'another manifestation of the "Big Society" approach of seeking local, preferably third-sector, alternatives to central government provision' (823). This third-sector involvement reflects the dominant neoliberal logic of reducing the role of the state in social provisioning and produces the veteran as a new recipient of charitable giving, but also as a customer. Thus, the masculinized image of veterans as deserving of state support competes with the feminized image of veterans as dependent on the charitable sector. The increasing reliance on a 'hybrid' third sector for support of veterans suggests that 'the civilian–military binary is better understood as an adaptive continuum' (Herman and Yarwood 2015, 2629). This reflects evolving civil–military relations which are shifting the responsibility for soldiers and veterans away from the government and onto the nation more broadly, as articulated in the UK Armed Forces Covenant, for example (Ingham 2014). In the UK the government's limited remit, and criticisms of veteran services generally (Lord Ashcroft 2014), has led to a substantial increase of third-sector involvement in veteran care. As an indication of the scale of charitable contribution to veteran services, the Royal British Legion alone spends approximately £1.4 million a week on 'wrap-around' services to supplement the provision of care by the National Health Service (House of Parliament 2011, 2).

Veterans have become highly visible in public life through charity campaigns, media coverage, films, and documentaries. For example, injured military personnel in Western state militaries have received unprecedented media coverage and public support (Achter 2010; Batts and Andrews 2011; Kelly 2013). Coverage of injured and disabled veterans typically depicts veterans conducting extraordinary feats in the context of sports competitions and charity fundraisers. The Invictus Games, an international sporting competition for injured servicemen and women established by Prince Harry in 2014, describes participants as:

> the men and women who have come face-to-face with the reality of making a sacrifice for their country … These people are the embodiment of everything the Invictus Games stands for. They have been tested and challenged, but they have not been overcome. (Invictus Games Foundation 2017)

However, these triumphant and heroic representations of veterans sit alongside representations of mental illness, alcoholism, homelessness, and destitution. There has been a particular focus on post-traumatic stress disorder (PTSD), for example in documentaries such as HBO's *War Torn 1861–2010* (directed by Jon Alpert and Ellen Goosenberg 2010), and the BBC's *Life After War: Haunted by Helmand* (directed by Michael Price 2013). In this sense, veterans are represented within polarizing frames which emphasize heroism or victimhood.

While the state discourse on military-to-civilian transition suggests the possibility of a smooth process, transition is fraught with difficulties for many veterans. As some veterans have explained, whilst they were trained to become soldiers they are not 'untrained' or unprogrammed from soldiering (Whelan 2014, 2016). The often 'warring identities' (Smith and True 2014) of soldier and veteran result in tensions (including in gender identity, see Demers 2013; Higate 2000) that can make 'effective' transition difficult. A veteran, by definition, is neither civilian nor military. Veterans inhabit, embody, and negotiate the space between those spheres, and while the concept of a 'transition' may imply a clean break, in practice we need to be attentive to the continuities and discontinuities in veterans' experiences (Higate 2001). As one US Army combat veteran puts it: 'Transition is Neverland, a mystical place where [sic] none of us who wore the uniform will ever see, because we had these periods of our life that just don't relate' (Duffy 2014).

There are significant tensions between military and civilian gender roles that create difficulties for veterans transitioning from military to civilian life (Burkhart and Hogan 2014; Gutierrez et al. 2013; Higate 2000). War is often associated with the masculinized ideal of the heroic warrior; however, men's military experiences can lead to health and social problems that undermine those very ideals of masculinity (Karner 1998; Higate 2000; Whitworth 2004; Finley 2011; Eichler 2012). As Eichler showed in her work on Russian veterans of the Chechen wars, Russian veterans often found it difficult to live up to civilian notions of masculinity such as being a dependable breadwinner and desirable husband. In the post-Soviet Russian context as well as in the Western context today, PTSD poses a serious obstacle for veterans trying to join the civilian workforce (Finley 2011). Veterans' economic marginalization makes it difficult for male veterans to live up to prevailing notions of masculinity that hinge on a man's success in the economy (Eichler 2012). They can struggle with accessing employment, housing, and health care. They are vulnerable citizens and in some ways occupy what is traditionally viewed as a 'feminized', dependent role within society, as recipients of benefits. On the other hand they are also the one subset of citizens who are not feminized by their dependency because they are seen as 'deserving' citizens as a result of their military service (Eichler 2015).

Female veterans face additional gender-specific challenges (Eichler 2016). Lack of societal recognition and support poses difficulties for female veterans who 'must struggle with what it means to be female in a society where civilians are perplexed by them and do not know whether to treat them "like one of the guys ... [or] like a lady"' (Demers 2013, 505). At the same time, gendered experiences of military service and norms of militarized masculinity can encourage women's premature departure from the military (Dichter and True 2015) or discourage female veterans from seeking help (Diramio et al. 2015). Western governments have been slow to develop female-specific veterans' policies and programmes. While the US Veterans Affairs system has begun to address gender-specific needs (National Center for Veterans Analysis and Statistics 2011), countries such as the UK and Canada are still lagging behind. For example, *The Veterans' Transition Review* (Ashcroft 2014), a 200-page report, fails to differentiate between men and women veterans at all.

In summary, it is clear that the transition from military to civilian life has become a core project of Western governments in the early twenty-first century. Governments recognize this project as important not only to mitigate the effects of war and military service, but to ensure the broader legitimacy of the armed forces and thus continued recruitment and retention. This suggests that the transition to civilian life is integral to the production of military force. The discourse of transition relies upon and reproduces clear distinctions between military and civilian spheres, and between military and civilian identities. Military and civilian spheres have different values and norms, and it is being suggested that veterans must actively 'become' functioning civilians. That is, it assumes that soldiers can and must be turned back into civilians. In reality, the transition from military to civilian life shows tensions, and a blurring of lines, between military and civilian spheres and identities. As such, we next suggest, military-to-civilian transition is a very productive site for feminist investigation.

Unmaking militarized masculinities: implications for feminist scholarship

As we outlined above, feminist scholarship has focused primarily on the making of militarized masculinities, and paid significantly less attention to the *un*making of militarized masculinities. We argue that an engagement with veterans' experiences – and specifically with the project of military-to-civilian transition – generates important insights which can help us better understand the complex dynamics of un/making gendered and militarized identities. A focus on veterans shows that militarized masculinities cannot be unmade in a straightforward way, and sheds light on how feminist scholars conceive of the making of militarized masculinity itself. Engagement with the unmaking of militarized masculinity can challenge feminist scholars to take seriously the experiences of veterans, to go beyond a privileging of their 'militarized' identities and to rethink militarization more broadly.

Dynamics of un/making militarized masculinities

Feminist scholars have done important work showing how veterans' return to civilian life reinforces societal gender inequalities (Ashe 2012). For example, Murray (2011, 84) has argued that post-World War II veteran benefits provided by the US GI Bill 'not only disadvantaged women – they reflected, reinforced, and further embedded traditional gender norms that positioned men as protectors and providers, and women as their homebound dependents'. The GI bill also had a negative impact on women's access to higher education and their overall economic and social status in the post-war era (Nagowski 2005). These examples show that militarized masculinities continue to shape societies long after conflicts have ended, and that militarized masculinity is not automatically 'undone' when veterans return home.

However, feminists have paid relatively little attention to the vast majority of veterans. Where feminists have examined veterans per se, the focus has tended to be on the failures and contradictions of militarized masculinity *or* the potential demilitarization of militarized masculinity. For example, Kilshaw (2009, 188) explains that veterans are 'unmanned' when they leave the military, and that war injuries such as Gulf War Syndrome must be understood within the negotiation of a new civilian identity perceived as lacking virility and masculinity. She argues that the symptoms experienced by Gulf War Syndrome sufferers, for example 'burning semen' (158–62) that veterans believed could transmit toxins to their wives, reflect a fear of their new 'leaky', porous, and vulnerable bodies, which in turn reflects their unease at the social boundaries that have become indistinct and insecure (82, see also chapters 3, 6, and 7). Whitworth's (2004) work on Canadian peacekeepers argues that it is the incongruence between the warrior image and men's actual lived experiences that contributes to PTSD and lays bare the contradictions and inherent fragility of militarized masculinity (Whitworth 2004, 166–7).

Sharoni (2008), on the other hand, has drawn on the stories of male war resisters to show how the process of demilitarizing militarized masculinities is both a political act and an act of 're-humanization' for the individual. She also argues that demilitarization must include resistance to other systems of oppression such as sexism, homophobia, and racism. Stur (2011) has documented how the veterans within the anti-Vietnam war movement in the United States openly challenged the ideal of the masculinized warrior and its connection with patriotism. Feminist scholars, however, have recognized that even this apparent demilitarization carries with it the dangers of glorifying anti-war veterans in ways that perpetuate 'the sort of masculinized privilege that nurtures militarism' (Cockburn and Enloe 2012, 553). Tidy (2015) productively complicates our understanding of the relationship between militarized and gendered subjectivity and anti-militarist dissent. She argues that the military peace movement is *constituted* through 'privileged, powerful hypermasculine dissenting veteran subjectivity' (456). Thus, the demilitarization – or unmaking – of militarized masculinity is made possible because of the militarized masculinity they seek to challenge. The unmaking of militarized masculinities is often incomplete, even within contexts of an explicit demilitarization. This signals a similar dynamic to that which we discussed earlier in relation to the archetype of militarized masculinity which can never be fully realized (Belkin 2012; Bulmer 2013, Forthcoming 2018; Welland 2013).

However, one limitation of feminist work is that it tends to suggest that militarized masculinity is an identity that one *has* – an identity that one has lost and is trying to regain, or that one has rejected but still benefits from. Feminists need to foreground the idea that, to many veterans, the link between masculinity and the military is not an idea but an experience, a practice, an identity, and an embodiment (Bulmer and Jackson 2016). For example, military norms of masculinity can be protective of mental health in veterans (Green et al. 2010) and this camaraderie and caring can enable veterans to develop peer support networks, countering the effects of PTSD (Caddick, Phoenix, and Smith 2015). Thus, militarized masculinity is very *present* in veterans' *civilian* lives – it is not simply something that they have 'lost'. The feminist focus on a 'lost' or demilitarized masculine identity reproduces a linear, and dichotomous, understanding of identity construction and its deconstruction, obscuring and oversimplifying the realities of veterans' lives.

Feminist scholarship has too often focussed on 'snapshots' of militarized masculinity at a given time and place, for example focusing on military training, deployment, or specific after-effects of deployment such as PTSD. However, militarized masculinity has a much longer 'after-life' that, if explored, would yield important insights about the ways in which it is embodied and lived *across a lifetime* (McSorley 2013; Sylvester 2013). Feminists have also failed to engage sufficiently with people's lives 'before' the adoption of a militarized identity.[3] This omission is significant because it posits military service as the defining activity of veterans' lives, and the assumption that veterans are forever beholden to their militarized identities, or are always already militarized. As a result, feminists miss a valuable opportunity to understand the dynamic nature of identity construction and deconstruction, across the life-course. Veteran identities are complex, ever-shifting, and sometimes contradictory; they resist categorization. If we only analyse veterans' experiences as a continuation of their militarized masculinity, or in relation to their struggles to hold onto it, we reify the privileging of the military identity in our own analyses, thus performatively reproducing the violences we seek to resist (Stern and Zalewski 2009). We also exceptionalize veterans' experiences, which leads us to underestimate the importance of the ordinary and civilian (Wool 2015b).

Beyond a privileging of militarized identity

The state project of unmaking militarized masculinity through 'successful' military-to-civilian transitions involves not just the relinquishing of one identity but the *active* construction of another one. There is an effort on the part of governments and societies to construct this civilian identity, while veterans are expected to 'acquire a new competence in the rules of civilian life' (Cooper et al. 2016, 8). The concept of militarized masculinity hinges on distinctions that continually marginalize and subordinate the everyday, 'ordinary' (Wool 2015a, 2015b), and civilian realm. This privileging of the militarized identity also reproduces the idea that the civilian realm is passive rather than active (and thereby associating it with the feminine) and non-militarized. However, the idea of the 'civilian' is fundamental to the constitution of any militarized identity, both discursively as its 'other', and concretely through the networks of discursive, financial, material, and emotional assemblages that constitute the social world in which war becomes possible.

A greater consideration not only of the legacy of military gender norms, but of the historically and spatially specific civilian gender norms that veterans encounter, is important. Veterans release from the military at particular times in the 'history of gender' (Enloe 2010, 4), and thus step into the context of specific societal gender orders and gendered state policies that impact their transition to civilian life. For example, during the twentieth century, Western rehabilitation practices after wars were fundamentally concerned with reconstructing the masculinity of men injured in war (Cohen 2001; Anderson 2011; Linker 2011; Gerber 2012; Kinder 2015). The need to restore injured men, who were often infantilized and feminized through their dependence on others, was primarily about reducing the cost to the state by enabling these men to return to work and support themselves (Cohen 2001; Anderson 2011; Linker 2011). In this sense the project of transforming a 'broken' militarized masculinity into a functioning civilian one was key to ensuring the sustainability of the domestic society and economy. In this context, interpretations based on rehabilitating 'lost' warrior masculinity obscure more complex political economies of war and civilian life. Similarly, if we consider the specific case of women veterans, we can also see how important civilian norms are for shaping their post-military lives. While women in the military and in combat are seen as exceptional (Mathers 2013; Chapman and Eichler 2014), female veterans often lack recognition in civilian society. Dominant norms of civilian femininity are typically viewed as always already feminized and non-militarized, making it difficult to recognize and represent female veterans *as veterans* (Eager 2014; Eichler 2016). It is perhaps not so much military gender norms but civilian gender norms that make the experiences of female veterans invisible. In this case the focus on a militarized identity can work to obscure more than it reveals.

Feminist analyses of representations of injured veterans that focus on militarized masculinity may also obscure the interaction between military and civilian norms. They have focused on the idea of the 'super crip' who overcomes his disability (which is feminizing) and therefore regains his lost masculinity (McRuer 2006; Tidy 2015; see also Caso 2016). However, it is striking that the photographic content of injured veterans in the UK, for example, has not been dominated by militarized symbols or motifs. On the contrary we find a 'domestication' (King 2010) of injured veterans wherein the coverage is not about their status as soldiers of the nation but is instead very individualized. This is achieved in several ways, including by minimizing references to the war that caused the injuries, photographing veterans in domestic settings in civilian clothing, and a focus on their family and personal journey (see, for example, imagery on the home page of the Help for Heroes website 2017). This explicit use of a civilian masculinity aesthetic within a discourse of military heroism is highly ambiguous, particularly in terms of its gendered content. Injured men are often pictured with their children in poses which suggest intimacy and emotional connectedness, traits which are typically associated with the feminine. Indeed, all representations of the war-wounded veteran body are themselves sites of conflicted meaning, suggesting both resilience and vulnerability, violence and peace, failure and triumph. Açksöz (2012, 20) argues that this is because injured veterans are 'simultaneously at the center and margins of hegemonic masculinity, valorized through the masculine ethos of nationalism, and violently expelled from the world of hegemonic masculinity'. However, we argue that this ambiguity is not solely about the contradictory locus of veterans who are at the centre *and* margins of militarized masculinity, but also about the constitution of the 'non-militarized' or civilian realm, such that it is possible to delineate it, a point we address next.

Beyond the military/civilian dichotomy

Transition discourses rely upon the idea of distinct realms, just as the tenets of civil–military relations in liberal democracies also depend on such distinctions (Huntington 1985; Feaver and Gelpi 2005). Militaries have often invoked their special status and their right to be 'different' from civilian society to justify the exclusion of certain people from militaries, or to explain military behaviours (Basham 2013). This suggests that the demarcation between these spheres is integral to the production of military force and that feminists should be very cautious about re-invoking it in their analyses of military power. The concept of 'militarized masculinity' necessarily implies an analytical distinction between militarized identities and those that are demilitarized or 'non-militarized' when such distinctions are, empirically, especially at the level of individual experience of veterans, very tenuous.

For Enloe (2000, 3, emphasis in original), militarization is a 'step-by-step process by which a person *or* a thing gradually comes to be controlled by the military or comes to depend for its well-being on militaristic ideas'. These processes are socially constructed and, therefore, 'what has been militarized can be demilitarized' (Enloe 2000, 291). This is not to suggest that feminist scholarship does not also recognize the complexity of processes of militarization and demilitarization and the ways in which these 'opposing forces might co-exist' within societies and institutions such as the military (Enloe 2007, 80). Based on this description of militarization we might conclude that veterans are clearly militarized by virtue of their previous role within the military, and their reliance on military pensions for their well-being. Indeed this assumption of a clear-cut militarized identity may explain why feminist scholars have paid so little analytical attention to the vast majority of veterans. However, the problem with this assumption of a militarized veteran identity is that it does not account for the ambiguities and tensions of lived experience which exceed such a straightforward categorization. For example, veterans may have an ambivalent attitude towards the military or the activities of that military, and yet remain proud of their service. Many British veterans suffering from Gulf War Syndrome blamed the military for making them sick and avoiding responsibility for that sickness, yet they remained 'fiercely loyal' to the military (Kilshaw 2009, 200). Similarly, Harel-Shalev and Daphna-Tekoah (2016, 187) have shown that by listening for contradictions and dilemmas, researchers can hear the ways in which female veterans both reinforce and challenge hegemonic discourses around military power. As these examples show, veterans can be simultaneously militarized and non/demilitarized.

But is it satisfactory for feminists to conclude that these oppositional processes may co-exist but are nevertheless empirically, and analytically, separate? Recent ethnographic work questions this mode of analysis in compelling ways. As MacLeish (2015, 18; see also 2013) argues in relation to his ethnography of military life at the US Army base Fort Hood, the effects and affects of war are generated through the complex interplay of multiple ever-shifting and precarious distinctions and categories which do not 'line up or nest neatly'. Accordingly, his ethnography 'departs from a systematic critique of political economy and ideology in which a monolithic notion of "militarization" serves as the ultimate explanation for all aspects of military life' (18). Similarly, Wool's (2015a, 24; see also Wool 2015b) study of injured US soldiers at Walter Reed Army Medical Center shows that 'logics of gender and sexuality, questions of personhood and the body, problems of recognition and flows of power cross-cut any boundaries between "military" and "society" that we might schematically draw'. For Wool, the mechanisms of war-making should be understood as 'coextensive with broader arrangements of social life rather than as intersecting or overlapping with distinguishable social spheres, like gender' (Wool 2015a, 23, our emphasis). It becomes difficult to effectively trace and articulate these coextensive relationships within the concept of militarized masculinity, as it requires us precisely to delineate what is militarized/masculine and what is not.

Relatedly, in a discussion of Enloe's work, Sylvester (2013) argues that militarization risks becoming 'bigger than life – a metanarrative like capitalism that permeates everything ... an abiding global rule; and that can seem both reductionist and essentialist' (44–5). Hautzinger and Scandlyn's (2014) concept of 'war as labyrinth' questions the compartmentalization that war creates:

> coming back from war entails dismantling the compartmentalization that war creates, between "us" and our "enemies", between "here" and "over there", between soldier and civilian, between "their" war and "our" war ... War as labyrinth defies separation and insulation: it means that global echoes of war's violence reverberate and affect us all, and that they necessarily follow combatants back home. (262)

We argue that the concept of militarized masculinity is part of the tendency to compartmentalize war within feminist scholarship, and that despite the best efforts of feminists, such a totalizing concept undermines our ability to engage with veterans and the complexities of their post-military lives.

For feminists to really be open to veterans' lived experiences they need to resist foreclosing them within taken-for-granted concepts such as militarized masculinity. As Enloe (2011, 142) has noted so well:

> we can forget that individuals are diverse, complex, hard-to-fathom creatures. It takes feminist listening, therefore, to take on board interviewees' contradictions, confusions and anxieties ... Feminist listening is not arrogant, however. That is it doesn't set the listener up as knowing more about what the speaker means than the speaker her/himself ... It takes feminist reflexivity to prevent our carrying away from such puzzling interviews ... the dangerous conclusion that we as researchers are somehow more coherent, more logical, and less vulnerable than our interviewees.

Veterans have often been subject to the objectifying gaze of researchers, policy-makers, and service-providers, which limits veterans' capacity to tell their own stories and in ways which do not pathologize them (Bulmer and Jackson 2016). This can also become a pitfall for feminist scholarship if militarized masculinity becomes the only lens through which we understand veterans' experiences. The challenge for feminists is to continuously reflect on our concepts and that includes confronting what they may obscure, limit, or erase. Our concern with the focus on making militarized masculinity is that it can tempt us to think that gendered experiences of militarization are neater and more coherent than they are – because when we look for militarized masculinity we can usually find it.

Conclusion

This article has demonstrated that the effective management of military-to-civilian transitions is a key project of twenty-first-century states in contemporary liberal democracies. Our aim has been to suggest that paying careful attention to this project of unmaking militarized masculinity may generate fruitful alternative avenues for feminist research on war, militarism, and gender. Understanding veterans' experiences of this process may help feminist scholars to more effectively trace the co-extensive, ever-shifting, and unstable assemblages of military and civilian life that are lived across a lifetime. Whilst the concept of militarized masculinity has offered important insights, it can also limit feminists' ability to engage with the complexity of veterans' experiences by privileging militarized identities and reproducing ideas of a linear making and unmaking of identity. Veterans' experiences show that the concept of militarized masculinity does not account for the co-existence and entanglement of masculinities and femininities across military and civilian spheres or the messiness and contradictions of lived embodiment. While feminist scholars have debated whether militarized masculinity can be reconstructed within militaries or whether the goal should be the demilitarization of masculinities, veterans complicate such a dichotomous choice. Instead, they illustrate that the unmaking of a militarized masculine identity is never complete, much as the archetype of militarized masculinity can never be fully achieved.

The lived experiences of veterans reflect the complex spaces between familiar feminist concepts, including militarized masculinity. But the limitations to the concept of militarized masculinity that we have identified go beyond its application to veterans. We hope to open up debate about the taken-for-granted validity of core feminist concepts such as militarized masculinity so that we might transform them in ways that more adequately engage the complexity and fluidity of the contemporary gendering of war and militarism. A key element of this agenda is to hold in focus, and work with and through, the 'inbetweenness' and co-extensiveness of military/civilian worlds and masculinities/femininities. Such a feminist research agenda requires new vocabularies, or, at a minimum, involves more reflection on how our concepts not only illuminate, but limit, what we can see.

Notes

1. In this article we refer to veterans as those who have been released from the military, whether or not they deployed during their military service. We limit our discussion to Western countries which typically have professional volunteer forces which engage in operations overseas. Our discussion does not extend to post-conflict situations in the global South, as these are very different contexts in terms of both the types of war and the organization and recruitment of armed forces. Usually called 'ex-combatants', veterans in societies which have been engaged in civil war face different challenges when integrating back into society, and pose different questions for feminist investigations (for example see MacKenzie 2012; Ní Aoláin, Haynes, and Cahn 2011).
2. Often these terms are used interchangeably when talking about gender within militaries, but we use the term 'militarized masculinity' in this article as we think it more adequately emphasizes that militarization is a process, and that it affects men and women outside of the military institution.
3. We thank Bethany Cuffe-Fuller for bringing this point to our attention.

Acknowledgements

We wish to acknowledge Faiz Sheik and Owen Thomas for reading several drafts of this paper at different stages of its development, and Timothy Cooper, Bethany Cuffe-Fuller, and Alexandra Hyde, who offered extensive comments on a later draft of this article. We also wish to thank the two anonymous reviewers for their encouraging and constructive feedback, as well as Kimberley Smith-Evans for help with copy-editing. Maya Eichler gratefully acknowledges funding received through a Social Sciences and Humanities Research Council of Canada Insight Grant (435-2016-1242) and the Canada Research Chair Program of the Canadian federal government during the writing of this article.

Disclosure statement

No potential conflict of interest was reported by the authors.

ORCID

Sarah Bulmer ⓘ http://orcid.org/0000-0001-8678-9273

References

Achter, P. 2010. Unruly bodies: The rhetorical domestication of twenty-first-century veterans of war. *Quarterly Journal of Speech* 96, no. 1: 46–68. doi:10.1080/00335630903512697

Açksöz, S.C. 2012. Sacrificial limbs of sovereignty: Disabled veterans, masculinity and nationalist politics in Turkey. *Medical Anthropology Quarterly* 26, no. 1: 4–25. doi:10.1111/j.1548-1387.2011.01194.x

Aiken, A., and A. Buitenhuis. 2011. Supporting Canadian veterans with disabilities: A comparison of financial benefits. Defence Management Studies Program, School of Policy studies, Queen's University in association with Canadian Institute for Military and Veterans Health Research. http://www.queensu.ca/cidp/publications/claxtonpapers/Claxton13.pdf

Anderson, J. 2011. *War, disability and rehabilitation in Britain*. Manchester: Manchester University Press.

Aoláin, N., D. Fionnuala, F. Haynes, and N. Cahn. 2011. *On the frontlines gender, war, and the post-conflict process*. New York: Oxford University Press.

Ashe, F. 2012. Gendering war and peace: Militarized masculinities in Northern Ireland. *Men and Masculinities* 15, no. 3: 230–48. doi:10.1177/1097184X12442636

Basham, V.M. 2013. *War, identity and the liberal state*. London: Routledge.

Basham, V.M. 2016. Gender, race, militarism and remembrance: The everyday geopolitics of the poppy. *Gender, Place and Culture: A Journal of Feminist Geography* 23, no. 6: 883–96. doi:10.1080/0966369X.2015.1090406

Batts, C., and D.L. Andrews. 2011. Tactical athletes': The United States paralympic military program and the mobilization of the disabled soldier/athlete. *Sport in Society* 14, no. 5: 553–68. doi:10.1080/17430437.2011.574350

Baudrillard, J. 1995. *The Gulf War did not take place*. Bloomington: Indiana University Press.

Belkin, A. 2012. *Bring me men: Military masculinity and the benign facade of empire 1898–2001*. London: Hurst & Co.

Brown, M. 2012. *Enlisting masculinity: The construction of gender in U.S. military recruiting advertising during the all-volunteer force*. Oxford; NY: Oxford University Press.

Brown, W.B. 2011. From war zones to jail: Veteran reintegration problems. *Justice Policy Journal* 8, no. 1: 1–48.

Brunger, H., J. Serrato, and J. Ogden. 2013. "No man's land": The transition to civilian life. *Journal of Aggression, Conflict and Peace Research* 5, no. 2: 86–100. doi:10.1108/17596591311313681

Bulmer, S. 2013. Patriarchal confusion? Making sense of gay and lesbian military identity. *International Feminist Journal of Politics* 15, no. 2: 137–56. doi:10.1080/14616742.2012.746565

Bulmer, S. Forthcoming 2018. *Queering the military: Sexuality in the armed forces.* London: Routledge.

Bulmer, S., and D. Jackson. 2016. "You do not live in my skin": Embodiment, voice and the veteran. *Critical Military Studies* 2, no. 1–2: 25–14. doi:10.1080/23337486.2015.1118799

Burkhart, L., and N. Hogan. 2014. Being a female veteran: A grounded theory of coping with transitions. *Social Work in Mental Health* 13, no. 2: 108–27. doi:10.1080/15332985.2013.870102

Butler, J. 1999. *Gender trouble: Feminism and the subversion of identity.* 2nd ed. London: Routledge.

Caddick, N., C. Phoenix, and B. Smith. 2015. Collective stories and well-being: Using a dialogical narrative approach to understand peer relationships among combat veterans experiencing PTSD. *Journal of Health Psychology* 20, no. 3: 286–99. doi:10.1177/1359105314566612

Caso, F. 2016. Sexing the disabled veteran: The homoerotic aesthetics of militarism. *Critical Military Studies* online early: 1–17. doi:10.1080/23337486.2016.1184420

Chapman, K., and M. Eichler. 2014. Engendering two solitudes? Media representations of women in combat in Quebec and the rest of Canada. *International Journal* 69, no. 4: 594–611. doi:10.1177/0020702014543708

Cockburn, C. 2010. Gender relations as causal in militarization and war: A feminist standpoint. *International Feminist Journal of Politics* 12, no. 2: 139–57. doi:10.1080/14616741003665169

Cockburn, C., and C. Enloe. 2012. Militarism, patriarchy and peace movements: Cynthia Cockburn and Cynthia Enloe in conversation. *International Feminist Journal of Politics* 14, no. 4: 550–57. doi:10.1080/14616742.2012.726098

Cohen, D. 2001. *The war come home.* Berkeley: University of California Press.

Cohn, C. 1998. Gays in the military: Texts and subtexts. In *The "man" question in international relations*, ed. Marysia Zalewski, and Jane L. Parpart, 129–49. Boulder: Westview Press.

Coker, C. 2002. *Waging war without warriors?: The changing culture of military culture.* Boulder: Lynne Rienner Publishers.

Conway, D. 2008. Contesting the masculine state. In *Rethinking the man question: Sex, gender and violence in international relations*, ed. Jane L. Parpart, and Marysia Zalewski, 127–42. London: Zed Books.

Conway, D. 2012. *Masculinities, militarisation and the end conscription campaign: War resistance in apartheid South Africa.* Manchester: Manchester University Press.

Cooper, L., N. Caddick, L. Godier, A. Cooper, and M. Fossey. 2016. Transition from the military into civilian life: An exploration of cultural competence. *Armed Forces & Society* online early: 1–22. doi:10.1177/0095327X16675965

Demers, A.L. 2013. From death to life: Female veterans, identity negotiation, and reintegration into society. *Journal of Humanistic Psychology* 53, no. 4: 489–515. doi:10.1177/0022167812472395

Department of National Defence and Canadian Armed Forces. 2016. Canadian Armed Forces transition services. http://www.forces.gc.ca/en/caf-community-support-services/caf-transition-services.page.

Department of Veteran Affairs. 2017. Veterans opportunity to work. http://www.benefits.va.gov/VOW/tap.asp.

Der Derian, J. 2001. *Virtuous War: Mapping the military-industrial-media-entertainment network.* Boulder and Oxford: Westview Press.

Dichter, M.E., and G. True. 2015. "This is the story of why my military career ended before it should have": Premature separation from military service among U.S. women veterans. *Affilia: Journal of Women & Social Work* 30, no. 2: 187–99. doi:10.1177/0886109914555219

Diramio, D., K. Jarvis, S. Iverson, C. Seher, and R. Anderson. 2015. Out from the shadows: Female student veterans and help-seeking. *College Student Journal* 49, no. 1: 49–68.

Duffy, E. 2014. What does the term "transition" really mean anyway? *Task & Purpose*, October 24. http://taskandpurpose.com/term-transition-really-mean-anyway/.

Duncanson, C. 2013. *Forces for good? Military masculinities and peacebuilding in Afghanistan and Iraq*. Basingstoke: Palgrave MacMillan.

Duncanson, C. 2015. Hegemonic masculinity and the possibility of change in gender relations. *Men and Masculinities* 18, no. 2: 231–48. doi:10.1177/1097184X15584912

Duncanson, C., and R. Woodward. 2016. Regendering the military: Theorizing women's military participation. *Security Dialogue* 47, no. 1: 3–21. doi:10.1177/0967010615614137

Eager, P.W. 2014. *Waging gendered wars: U.S. military women in Afghanistan and Iraq*. London: Ashgate.

Eichler, M. 2012. *Militarizing men: Gender, conscription and war in Post–Soviet Russia*. Stanford: Stanford University Press.

Eichler, M. 2015. The struggle over veterans policy: Neoliberalism, the third sector, and the new veterans movement. Paper presented at the Canadian Political Science Association Annual Conference, June 2–4, Ottawa,ON, Canada.

Eichler, M. 2016. Add female veterans and stir? A feminist perspective on gendering veterans research. *Armed Forces and Society* online early: 1–21. doi:10.1177/0095327X16682785

Enloe, C. 1988. Beyond 'rambo': Women and the varieties of militarized masculinity. In *Women and the military system*, ed. Eva Isaksson, 71–92. New York: St. Martin's Press.

Enloe, C. 2000. *Manoeuvres: The international politics of militarizing women's lives*. Berkeley: University of California Press.

Enloe, C. 2007. *Globalization and militarism: Feminists male the link*. Lanham: Rowman & Littlefield Publishers.

Enloe, C. 2010. *Nimo's war, Emma's war: Making feminist sense of the Iraq war*. Berkeley: University of California Press.

Enloe, C. 2011. When feminists explore masculinities in IR: An engagement with Maya Eichler. In *Feminism and international relations: Conversations about the past, present and future*, ed. J. Ann Tickner, and Laura Sjoberg, 141–45. New York: Routledge.

Feaver, P.D., and C. Gelpi. 2005. *Choosing your battles: American civil-military relations and the use of force*. Princeton: Princeton University Press.

Finley, E. 2011. *Fields of combat: Understanding PTSD among veterans of Iraq and Afghanistan*. Ithaca, NY: Cornell University Press.

Forces in Mind Trust (FiMT). 2013. The transition mapping study: Understanding the transition process for service personnel returning to civilian life. August. http://www.fim-trust.org/news/21-news/64-transition-mapping-study-report.

Gerber, D.A., ed. 2012. *Disabled veterans in history*. Revised ed. Ann Arbor: University of Michigan Press.

Goldstein, J.S. 2001. *War and gender: How gender shapes the war system and vice versa*. Cambridge: Cambridge University Press.

Green, G., C. Emslie, D.O. O'Neill, K. Hunt, and S. Walker. 2010. Exploring the ambiguities of masculinity in accounts of emotional distress in the military among young ex-servicemen. *Social Science & Medicine* 71, no. 8: 1480–88. doi:10.1016/j.socscimed.2010.07.015

Gutierrez, P.M., L.A. Brenner, J.A. Rings, M.D. Devore, P.J. Kelly, P.J. Staves, … M.S. Kaplan. 2013. A qualitative description of female veterans' deployment-related experiences and potential suicide risk factors. *Journal of Clinical Psychology* 69, no. 9: 923–35. doi:10.1002/jclp.21997

Harel-Shalev, A., and D.-T. Shir. 2016. Bringing women's voices back in: Conducting narrative analysis in IR. *International Studies Review* 18, no. 2: 171–94. doi:10.1093/isr/viv004

Hautzinger, S., and J. Scandlyn. 2014. *Beyond post-traumatic stress: Homefront struggles with the wars on terror*. Walnut Creek: Left Coast Press.

Help for Heroes. 2017. Homepage of website. http://www.helpforheroes.org.uk/.

Herbert, M.S. 1998. *Camouflage isn't only for combat: Gender, sexuality, and women in the military*. New York: New York University Press.

Herman, A., and R. Yarwood. 2015. From warfare to welfare: Veterans, military charities and the blurred spatiality of post-service welfare in the United Kingdom. *Environment and Planning A* 47: 2628–44. doi:10.1177/0308518X15614844

Higate, P.R. 2000. Ex-servicemen on the road: Travel and homelessness. *Sociological Review* 48, no. 3: 331–47. doi:10.1111/1467-954X.00219

Higate, P.R. 2001. Theorizing continuity: From military to civilian life. *Armed Forces & Society* 27, no. 3: 443–60. doi:10.1177/0095327X0102700306

Higate, P.R., ed. 2003. *Military masculinities: Identity and the state*. Westport, CT: Praeger.

House of Parliament. 2011. 'Explosive injury' POSTnote, number 395. December. www.parlia ment.uk/briefing-papers/POST-PN-395.pdf.

Hunt, A.E. 1996. *The turning: A history of Vietnam veterans against the war*. New York: New York University Press.

Huntington, S.P. 1985. *The soldier and the state: The theory and politics of civil-military relations*. Cambridge, MA: The Belknap Press of Harvard University Press.

Ingham, S. 2014. *The military covenant: Its impact on civil–military relations in Britain*. London: Ashgate.

Invictus Games Foundation. 2017. Our story. https://invictusgamesfoundation.org/foundation/story.

Iversen, A., V. Nikolaou, N. Greenberg, C. Unwin, L. Hull, M. Hotopf, C. Dandeker, J. Ross, and S. Wessely. 2005. What happens to British veterans when they leave the armed forces? *European Journal of Public Health* 15, no. 2: 175–84. doi:10.1093/eurpub/cki128

Kaldor, M. 1999. *New and old wars: Organized violence in a global era*. Cambridge: Polity.

Karner, T.X. 1998. Engendering violent men: Oral histories of military masculinity. In *Masculinities and violence*, ed. Lee H. Bowker, 197–232. Thousand Oaks: Sage Publications.

Kelly, J. 2013. Popular culture, sport and the 'hero'-fication of British militarism. *Sociology* 47, no. 4: 722–38. doi:10.1177/0038038512453795

Kilshaw, S. 2009. *Impotent warriors: Gulf war syndrome, vulnerability and masculinity*. Oxford: Berghahn Books.

Kinder, J.M. 2015. *Paying with their bodies: American war and the problem of the disabled veteran*. Chicago: Chicago University Press.

King, A. 2010. The Afghan War and 'postmodern' memory: Commemoration and the dead of Helmand. *The British Journal of Sociology* 61, no. 1: 1–25. doi:10.1111/(ISSN)1468-4446

Klein, U. 2003. The military and masculinities in Israeli society. In *Military masculinities: Identity and the state*, ed. Paul R. Higate, 191–200. London: Praeger.

Life After War: Haunted by Helmand. Directed by Michael Price. London: BBC, 2013

Linker, B. 2011. *War's waste: Rehabilitation in World War I America*. Chicago: University of Chicago Press.

Lord Ashcroft, K.C.M.G.P.C. 2014. The veterans' transition review. February. http://www.veter anstransition.co.uk/vtrreport.pdf.

Luttwak, E.N. 1995. Toward post-heroic warfare. *Foreign Affairs* 74, no. 3: 109–22. doi:10.2307/ 20047127

MacKenzie, M.H. 2012. *Female soldiers in Sierra Leone: Sex, security, and post-conflict development*. New York: New York University Press.

MacLeish, K. 2015. The ethnography of good machines. *Critical Military Studies* 1, no. 1: 11–22. doi:10.1080/23337486.2014.973680

MacLeish, K.T. 2013. *Making war at fort hood: Life and uncertainty in a military community*. Princeton: Princeton University Press.

Mankayi, N. 2006. Male constructions and resistance to women in the military. *Scientia Militaria: South African Journal of Military Studies* 34, no. 2: 44–64. doi:10.5787/34-2-23

Mathers, J.G. 2013. Women and state military forces. In *Women and wars*, ed. C. Cohn, 124–145. Cambridge: Polity.

Mcclintock, A. 1995. *Imperial leather: Race, gender, and sexuality in the colonial contest*. New York: Routledge.

McCready, A.L. 2013. *Yellow ribbons: The militarization of national identity in Canada*. Black Point: Fernwood Publishing.

McRuer, R. 2006. *Crip theory: Cultural signs of queerness and disability.* New York: New York Press.

McSorley, K., ed. 2013. *War and the body: Militarisation, practice and experience.* London: Routledge.

Ministry of Defence. 2011. *The armed forces covenant.* London. https://www.gov.uk/government/uploads/system/uploads/attachment_data/file/49469/the_armed_forces_covenant.pdf (accessed February 16, 2017).

Ministry of Defence. 2012. Defence recovery and personnel recovery centres. https://www.gov.uk/guidance/defence-recovery-and-personnel-recovery-centres.

Ministry of Defence. 2013. Defence medical services. https://www.gov.uk/defence-medical-services#defence-medical-rehabilitation-centre-dmrc-headley-court.

Mumford, A. 2012. Veteran care in the United Kingdom and the sustainability of the 'military covenant. *The Political Quarterly* 83, no. 4: 820–26. doi:10.1111/poqu.2012.83.issue-4

Murray, M. 2011. Made with men in mind: The GI Bill and its reinforcement of gendered work after World War II. In *Feminist Legal History: Essays on Women and Law*, T. A. Thomas, and T. J. Boisseau eds., 85–99. New York: NYU Press.

Nagowski, M.P. 2005. Inopportunity of gender: The G.I. Bill and the higher education of the American female, 1939–1954. PhD diss., Cornell University.

National Center for Veterans Analysis and Statistics. 2011. *America's women veterans: Military service history and VA benefit utilization statistics.* Washington, DC: National Center for Veterans Analysis and Statistics, Department of Veterans Affairs.

Orford, A. 2003. *Reading humanitarian intervention: Human rights and the use of force in international law.* Cambridge: Cambridge University Press.

Parpart, J., and K. Partridge. 2014. Soldiering on: Pushing militarized masculinities into new territory. In *The SAGE handbook of feminist theory*, ed. Mary Evans, Clare Hemmings, Marsha Henry, Hazel Johnstone, Sumi Madhok, Ania Plomien, and Sadie Wearing, 550–65. London: Sage.

Parpart, J.L. 2015. Militarized masculinities, heroes and gender inequality during and after the nationalist struggle in Zimbabwe. *NORMA: International Journal for Masculinity Studies* 10, no. 3–4: 212–325. doi:10.1080/18902138.2015.1110434

Peterson, V.S., ed. 1992. *Gendered states: Feminist (re)visions of international relations theory.* Boulder: Lynne Rienner.

Razack, S.H. 2004. *Dark threats and white knights: The Somalia affair, peacekeeping, and the new imperialism.* Buffalo, NY: University of Toronto Press.

Runyan, A.S. 1990. Gender relations and the politics of protection. *Peace Review: A Journal of Social Justice* 2, no. 4: 28–31. doi:10.1080/10402659008425571

Sasson-Levy, O. 2003. Feminism and military gender practices: Israeli women soldiers in "masculine" roles. *Sociological Enquiry* 73, no. 3: 440–65. doi:10.1111/1475-682X.00064

Sayer, N.A., R.J. Patricia Frazier, M.M. Orazem, K.F. Amy Gravely, S.H. Carlson, and S. Noorbaloochi. 2011. Military to civilian questionnaire: A measure of postdeployment community reintegration difficulty among veterans using Department of Veterans Affairs medical care. *Journal of Traumatic Stress* 24, no. 6: 660–70. doi:10.1002/jts.20706

Scheipers, S., ed. 2014. *Heroism and the changing character of war: Toward post-heroic warfare?* Basingstoke: Palgrave Macmillan.

Sharoni, S. 2008. De-militarizing masculinities in the Age of Empire. *Austrian Political Science Journal* 37, no. 2: 147–64.

Sjoberg, L. 2013. *Gendering global conflict: Towards a feminist theory of war.* New York: Columbia University Press.

Sjoberg, L., and C. Gentry. 2007. *Mothers, monsters, whores: Women's violence in global politics.* London: Zed Books.

Smith, R.T., and G. True. 2014. Warring identities: Identity conflict and the mental distress of American veterans of the wars in Iraq and Afghanistan. *Society and Mental Health* 2, no. 2: 147–61. doi:10.1177/2156869313512212

Stahl, R. 2009. Why we "support the troops": Rhetorical evolutions. *Rhetoric & Public Affairs* 12, no. 4: 533–70. doi:10.1353/rap.0.0121

Stern, M., and M. Zalewski. 2009. Feminist fatigue(s): Reflections on feminism and familiar fables of militarisation. *Review of International Studies* 35, no. 3: 611–30. doi:10.1017/S0260210509008675

Stur, H.M. 2011. *Beyond combat: Women and gender in the Vietnam War era*. Cambridge: Cambridge University Press.

Sylvester, C. 2013. *War as experience: Contributions from international relations and feminist analysis*. London: Routledge.

Tickner, A.J. 2001. *Gendering world politics: Issues and approaches in the post-Cold War era*. New York: Columbia University Press.

Tidy, J. 2015. Gender, dissenting subjectivity and the contemporary military peace movement in body of war. *International Feminist Journal of Politics* 17, no. 3: 454–72. doi:10.1080/14616742.2014.967128

Titunik, R.F. 2008. The myth of the macho military. *Polity* 40, no. 2: 137–16. doi:10.1057/palgrave.polity.2300090

van Hoorn, L.A., N. Jone, W. Busuttil, N.T. Fear, S. Wessely, E. Hunt, and N. Greenberg. 2013. Iraq and Afghanistan veteran presentations to combat stress, since 2003. *Occupational Medicine* 63: 238–41. doi:10.1093/occmed/kqt017

Veterans Affairs Canada. 2016. Services. http://www.veterans.gc.ca/eng/services.

Veterans UK. 2017. About us. https://www.gov.uk/government/organisations/veterans-uk/about.

War Torn 1867–2010. Directed by Joh Alpert and Ellen Goosenberg. New York: HBO, 2010.

Welland, J. 2013. Militarised violences, basic training, and the myths of asexuality and discipline. *Review of International Studies* 39, no. 4: 881–902. doi:10.1017/S0260210512000605

Whelan, J.J. 2014. *Going crazy in the green machine: The story of trauma and PTSD among Canada's veterans*. Victoria: Friesen Press.

Whelan, J.J. 2016. *Ghosts in the ranks: Forgotten voices and military mental health*. Victoria: Friesen Press.

Whitworth, S. 2004. *Men, militarism and UN peacekeeping: A gendered analysis*. Boulder: Lynne Rienner.

Woodward, R., and T. Winter. 2007. *Sexing the soldier: The politics of gender and the contemporary British army*. Abingdon: Routledge.

Wool, Z.H. 2015a. Critical military studies, queer theory, and the possibilities of critique: The case of suicide and family caregiving in the US military. *Critical Military Studies* 1, no. 1: 23–37. doi:10.1080/23337486.2014.964600

Wool, Z.H. 2015b. *After war: The weight of life at walter reed*. Durham: Duke University Press.

Young, I.M. 2003. The logic of masculinist protection: Reflections on the current security state. *Signs: Journal of Women in Culture and Society* 29, no. 1: 1–25. doi:10.1086/375708

Problematizing military masculinity, intersectionality and male vulnerability in feminist critical military studies

Marsha Henry

ABSTRACT

Recent work on the multiplicity of masculinities within specific military contexts deploys the concept of intersectionality in order to draw attention to the hierarchies present in military organizations or to acknowledge male vulnerability in situations of war and conflict. While it is important to examine the breadth and depth of masculinity as an ideology and practice of domination, it is also important for discussions of military masculinity, and intersectionality, to be connected with the 'originary' black feminist project from which intersectionality was born. This may indeed reflect a more nuanced and historically attuned account of such concepts as intersectionality, but also black and double consciousness, standpoint and situated knowledges. In particular, what happens when concepts central to feminist theorizing and activism suddenly become of use for studying dominant groups such as male military men? What are our responsibilities in using these concepts in unexpected and perhaps politically questionable ways? This article looks at recent feminist theorizing on intersectionality, and several examples of the use of intersectionality in relation to masculinity and the military, and finally suggests some cautionary ways forward for rethinking militaries, masculinities, and feminist theories.

Introduction

In June 2015, I attended a workshop hosted by the University of Newcastle on the subject of military masculinities, organized by a group of feminist scholars interested in drawing connections between critical military studies (CMS) and feminist international relations (FIR). The main theme 'masculinities at the margins' was the organizing focus and enabled those presenting and participating in the workshop to discuss how, by looking to the margins of war, scholars and civil society organizations might refocus/ better understand the role and effects of gender in practices of war. When I arrived at the small workshop, I met a group of familiar faces from a growing feminist critical military studies (FCMS) community. The air was immediately comfortable and I began to catch up with old friends and colleagues, and was introduced to new scholars and activists with an interest in gender and militarization. As the workshop began, I sat at the back of a long, curved room and looked around. What I noticed is that there were very few, bar myself, scholars of colour/black and ethnic minority researchers attending the workshop. While in the context of academia this is not an uncommon demographic, the absence of black women scholars reoccurred as an issue in my mind as a range of gendered topics and issues arose over the two days, including a consistent interest in and dwelling on the concept of intersectionality. The geopolitical scope of the workshop was somewhat broad, and scholars travelled from, and presented on a range of work in progress dealing with the contexts such as Northern Ireland, Rwanda and the Middle East. While none of the presenters were centrally concerned with 'race' in their research, critical issues concerning ethnicity and 'race' were raised in a more indirect way. For example, the concept of intersectionality emerged in two significant ways in a variety of discussions: first as a sensitizing prompt for thinking about multiple forms of difference in the study of gendered identities within the military; and, second, in order to understand the unequal and vulnerable position of 'marginal' militarized men within certain militarized settings. However, what was also particularly interesting was that intersectionality was used to present material on men as subjects of research and analyses. Despite this attention to the nuances of identity and power relations within military subcultures, there was not a specific focus on understanding the position of black and minority women in national militaries (Crenshaw 1989, 1991). However, this is not just a feature of this particular workshop. Instead, this is seen throughout the literature on gender and international relations which takes up intersectionality as a concept (Wibben 2016; Ackerly and True 2008), as well as in the empirical case studies on black women's experiences of the military – which are few and far between. As such, 'intersectionality without black women' or what Carbado refers to as 'colorblind inter-sectionality' became a central feature and point of discussion within the workshop (Carbado 2013).

This experience has led me to critically assess the use of intersectionality within FCMS and other fields of study more generally. I argue for a cautionary approach to using intersectionality in studies of international relations and militarized men that do not *also* include a focus on poor black women. In particular, I (re)politicize intersec-tionality for FCMS, drawing attention to the problems raised by utilizing theories of oppression in sites of privileged empirical research and epistemic power. After the workshop, I grew concerned that there was an emerging and problematic appropriation of the concept of intersectionality in FCMS and that this was contributing to a space in which *privilege is covered over*, rather than *revealed* and *challenged*. The very fact of such a limited presence of black feminist scholars at the workshop suggests that perhaps the concept of intersectionality has become detached from identity politics and those racialized subjects for whom it was written. Additionally, the use of intersectionality to discuss gendered experiences within a globally hegemonic, male-dominated, andro-centric and misogynist military; an increasing focus on differences amongst and between men rather than on male privilege and power; and, finally, to theorize masculinity and men's experiences in conflict zones as quintessentially or even essen-tially vulnerable, made me realize that some interrogation of the uses (and abuses) of intersectionality within the field of FCMS needed to be developed and shared with a wider academic community.

The article is organized as follows: first, I outline some key themes and issues raised in theorizing intersectionality more generally. Following on from this, I introduce at least two ways in which the concept of military masculinity might be understood, and link this to the idea of multiple differences (influenced by a sensitivity to intersectionality). I then identify some of the problems of using intersectionality in 'privileged' military contexts and contrast this with some empirical examples from recent research to demonstrate why it is important to use intersectionality with caution. I argue, through examining non-traditional militarized contexts such as peacekeeping, that while intersectionality can sensitize us to differences, it cannot be a proxy for challenging the hegemonic position of militarized men vis-à-vis women in a variety of social contexts.

Introducing intersectionality: what relevance for feminist critical military studies?

Intersectionality is a concept, theory, and lens developed in large part by black feminist scholar Kimberlé Crenshaw over 25 years ago (Crenshaw 1989, 1991). In particular, Crenshaw developed her ideas on the unique experiences of poor and working-class black women in the US context, through the influence of feminist standpoint theory (Collins 1986, 1989; Smith 1987; Harding 1986; Haraway 1988), black feminist thought, and critical race studies. Crenshaw highlighted in her seminal 1989 piece 'Demarginalising the Intersection of Race and Sex' the ways in which multiple axes of difference can intersect for some individuals (poor black women in particular), thereby compounding experiences of discrimination, marginalization, and, importantly, oppression (Crenshaw 1989). Crenshaw's original articulation focussed specifically on poor black women, but was never prescriptive or territorial. That is, Crenshaw did not prescribe that intersectionality as a concept needed to be used in any particular way, or that it could *only* be applied to poor black women in the US. Rather, Crenshaw's theorization stemmed from her own social position as a black woman in the US, and was influenced by the work of other black feminists who theorized black women's everyday life and unique standpoint (Lorde 1984; hooks 1984; Collins 2000), and women of colour on the margins and borders (Anzaldúa 2007; Moraga and Anzaldúa 1983; Lugones and Spelman 1993), and later by those taking up intersectionality in a more transnational manner (Brah and Phoenix 2004; Alexander and Mohanty 1997; Grewal and Kaplan 1994; Anthias and Yuval-Davis 1992; Hancock 2016).

Since Crenshaw debuted intersectionality in 1989/1991, there have been a number of critically important responses and attempts to expand the theorization. Some notable developments include intersectionality not only as a field of study but as an analytical strategy or sensitivity (Cho, Crenshaw, and McCall 2013), a buzzword that should be used with caution (Davis 2008), a methodology (McCall 2005), and a research paradigm (Hancock 2007). The expansion of the field of intersectionality has also seen its way into FIR in particular with the publication of Ackerly, Stern, and True's 2006 book *Feminist Methodologies for International Relations* and Wibben's recent edited collection *Researching War: Feminist Methods, Ethics and Politics*. Furthermore, the subject has been taken up within feminist political science more generally (Fernandes 2015; Murib and Zoss 2015; Lewis 2009, 2013). In this sense, intersectionality is fast becoming a centrally important concept to be used within a range of feminist scholarship, and thus it is not surprising to see it emerging in the burgeoning fields of CMS or FCMS.

Despite the growing visibility of intersectionality in gender and IR, the concept has remained surprisingly absent in studies of military personnel, and in military sociology which is so oft concerned with stratification, hierarchies, and order within military organizations. Work paying attention to women and ethnic minority integration into regular forces has grown in the US, UK, Canada, Australia, New Zealand, South Africa, and Israel – however, this literature does not generally engage directly with feminist theories of intersectionality. In related fields of feminist peace research, feminist scholars such as Cynthia Cockburn have had a greater interest in, and return to, feminist and gender theories such as standpoint (Cockburn 2010), experience (Kronsell and Svedberg 2012; Sylvester 2013), intersectionality (Ackerly and True 2008), and masculinity (Zarkov 2011; Duncanson 2015). This body of work suggests that feminist and gender theories can move across and between disciplines and fields of study and help to *continually challenge power relations* at work within militarized and male-dominated contexts and processes.

Importantly, little of the intersectional 'turn' in FIR and now FCMS has paid attention to contemporary critiques and cautionary tales in intersectionality as a field of study itself, as my reflections of the workshop highlight and which is demonstrated in the absence of the term in early FIR work. However, two recent trends in responding to the expansion of academic scholarship on intersectionality are worth discussing in more detail here. The first main criticism is the invisibility or erasure of black women in intersectionality research (Jordan-Zachery 2013). This is where intersectionality is invoked to understand women's multiple oppressions, but black women are directly or indirectly re-marginalized . That is, black women never feature as the central category or group of women under study. The second critique is that referred to as 'feminist originalism' where a tendency to possess intersectionality and dictate where and when it should be deployed within feminist research is seen to be a backlash against the more frequent application of intersectionality (Falcón and Nash 2015; Nash 2016). Several scholars writing on intersectionality have suggested that the concept is increasingly used in contexts where the history of the concept is unacknowledged, black women scholars or intersectionality theorists are not acknowledged or cited, and/or black women are eclipsed within the research and analysis (Carbado 2013; Jordan-Zachery 2013; Tomlinson 2013; Bilge 2013; Collins and Bilge 2016). What good is intersectionality, then, if it is used in such an exclusive manner? This is a point I take up later in the article in relation to how we might understand the limits of intersectionality and the ethical and political consequences of using intersectionality in FIR and FCMS.

In what ways should intersectionality be used? Is it acceptable, for example, for intersectionality to be utilized where its political and historical roots have not been appropriately acknowledged? I argue that it is disingenuous and highly problematic to use intersectionality merely as a way of capturing multiple differences and their effects on individuals. Intersectionality is centrally about *intersecting oppressions* or systems of oppression (Crenshaw 1989, 1991). It is already plural and it is interested in the points of intersection, not just the additive or cumulative effects of adding together differences.

In contrast, feminist scholars such as Nash have argued that an *origin narrative* of intersectionality has emerged, where the concept becomes territorialized in such a way that it is seen to belong only to certain 'authentic' spaces and disciplines. Some scholars suggest that intersectionality should not be exported beyond its original setting – and it is this that Nash takes issue with (Nash 2016). This would mean that intersectionality would always need to be tied to the study of poor black women, and this was never Crenshaw's explicit wish. Nash's evaluation of responses to intersectionality suggest that the concept itself is not benign. Rather, there is a politics to the use of intersectionality itself. In this way, intersectionality is more than a 'buzz-word'; as Davis argues, it is a whole field of theory and politics (Davis 2008). This does not mean that intersectionality can only be used to study a very limited range of individuals; rather, what it suggests is that when 'radical' or revolutionary theories of emancipation (from patriarchy, capitalism, and racism) become detached from those marginalized within these very structures of power, they may end up serving the interests of the ruling class (Hartsock 1983).

In this section I have briefly outlined the central meaning and use of intersectionality, suggested its adoption into relevant fields such as FIR, and detailed some of the ways in which intersectionality has been further theorized and challenged by a range of scholars. In the remaining sections I intend to return to these issues and debates in regard to militarized contexts more generally.

From military masculinity to militarized masculinities

The purpose of the section is to better understand how scholars use military masculinity. While the concept has been pluralized and used critically across a range of work within IR, political and military sociology, anthropology, geography, organizational studies, gender studies, and CMS, it has taken varied forms in the transnational and global research on gender and militarization over the years (Enloe 2006; Titunik 2008; Higate 2003; Dietrich Ortega 2012; Belkin 2012). While it has helped scholars to explain gendered practices within a range of militarized contexts, currently it is predominantly used to explain *contradictory* practices. The most recent conceptualization focuses on the ways in which military masculinities are formed based on challenging and colluding gender norms and expectations (Amar 2011, 2013; Atherton 2014; Duncanson 2013, 2015; Henry 2015; Peteet 2000). In fact, the workshop attempted to engage with the complex range of masculinities present inside the margins of the military as an institution and subcultural field. Recent work on military masculinities includes research on conscientious objection and fratriarchal bonding, to acts of torture, and ranges to include vigilantism – demonstrating that military masculinity is pliable, plural, and practised in contingent and contradictory ways in many empirical contexts (Higate 2012; Conway 2012; de Silva 2014). Despite its temporal and spatial flexibility, military masculinity is now ubiquitous in academic scholarship, and I discuss three issues with military masculinity as a starting point for further discussions about intersectionality.

First, two key works have influenced the development of the concept of militarized masculinity and masculinities, and I acknowledge the specific contribution of two scholars. Enloe has encouraged scholars to pay attention to the process of militarization rather than focus narrowly on the ideology of militarism, in her ground-breaking work on gender and international relations (Enloe 1994). In her work, Enloe develops further her concept of military masculinity when thinking about the ways in which military institutions are sites of the production of both culture and gender. Here she suggests that gender roles are given opportunity and space to play out, as well as to produce extremes – hyper military masculinity being one example. She also points to the ways in which certain forms of martiality (exclusively associated with men) are hyper-valued within most societies and how this contributes to the glorification of men's participation in violence and war. In thinking about military masculinity, it is not surprising, then, that feminist scholars such as Enloe began to think about the *process* of socializing that takes place in militarized settings (Enloe 1983, 1989, 2000). Thus, the social, constructed, contingent, fluid, and multiple ways in which individuals are produced as gendered subjects, given a prescribed set of gendered roles, and how those individuals identify themselves and perform gender within military institutions and settings has been afforded critical attention (Enloe 2000; Whitworth 2004; Higate 2003; Parpart 2015; Zalewski and Parpart 1998; Belkin 2012).

Early conceptualizations of military masculinity focussed almost exclusively on formal military settings – that is, on national and state militaries. In general, military masculinity tends to be utilized in a range of feminist scholarship as a 'thing' that is carried, possessed, or produced as an object through military socialization and found within military culture (except Enloe 2002). As such, it was seen, in the early inception, as a singular form of gendered practice – following on from Connell's early conceptualizations of hegemonic masculinity (Connell 1987, 1995; Connell and Messerschmidt 2005). Of course, the ways in which military masculinity has evolved as a conceptual lens and a site for empirical research mean that there is no single definition, nor is it confined to feminist theorists alone. Military institutions now consistently analyse their own gendered and racialized cultures – although very often this is for improving efficiency and effectiveness in military operations. Further theorizations include those of Dudink, Hagemann, and Tosh (2004), Zalewski and Parpart (2008), Belkin (2012), Whitworth (2004), Masters (2005), and Duncanson (2009, 2013, 2015). However, it was Paul Higate's edited collection (2003) that took up the challenge of further theorizing military masculinity. In particular, the work engages with Connell and other masculinity scholars and succeeded in pluralizing militarized masculinity. This work expanded the concept in such a way that scholars no longer talked about masculinity within military settings as something culturally specific, socially entrenched, pathological, or always already there in the same form – rather, Higate's collection emphasizes how men [sic] become 'manly' warriors through twin processes of gender and military socialization (Higate 2003). The 2003 collection suggests that it is difficult to simply place the military and masculinity (in an additive way) together – rather, both are mutually constituting. At times, in analyses it is difficult to pinpoint which is more influential – military culture or gender culture! Importantly, Higate's collection began to pave the way for thinking about militarized masculinities in non-traditional contexts. Thus, work on masculinity amongst rebel groups, militias, gangs, thugs, terrorists, and jihadis began to be developed within this sub-field (Amar 2013; Rommell 2016). This challenged the idea that military values only belonged to fields where there was a formal military setting. More contemporary work is concerned with the drone operator, the military lawyer, the conscious objector, and so on (Tidy 2016).

These two tracks of argument have been absolutely crucial to the conceptualization and use of the term military/militarized masculinity/masculinities. This is because militarized masculinities mean that the fluid nature of militarization and masculine socialization in these frames allows scholars to focus on masculinities in practice and discourse. Rather than using militarized masculinity as an explanation for various negative developments within military settings, scholars are encouraged to probe deeper into what militarized masculinities look like and how they come into being. For example, in Stern and Ericsson-Baaz's study of perpetrators of sexual violence, they focus on the discourses perpetrators of sexual violence in the DRC construct as to their different motivations for such acts of brutality (Baaz and Stern 2009, 2013). In their research, they pay attention to the narrative strategies used by men to construct and produce themselves as fearsome and honourable military men despite admitting to being part of the perpetration of violence. Similarly, Lomsky-Feder and Rapoport in their work on models of masculinity in the Israeli context demonstrate the influence of nation on men's different constructions of masculinity (Lomsky-Feder and Rapoport 2003). Lomsky-Feder and Rapoport view masculinities as being produced hierarchically in one military context, and as being influenced by very different military experiences (Israel and Russia). Both of these scholars' use of militarized masculinity provide us with a more complex account of what motivates men to commit violence (organized or otherwise) in certain contexts, rather than assume that it is merely an unintended consequence or unintentional byproduct of male embodiment or male sex roles and military culture.

Thus, the work of Cynthia Enloe in challenging understandings of militarization, and Higate's edited collection on militarized masculinities, were a catalyst for rethinking military masculinities and masculinities in conflict (Kirby and Henry 2012). This is turn led to the development of work examining a range of masculinities within militarized (and not only military) settings – in particular, Belkin's work *Bring Me Men* was seminal in challenging the idea that military masculinity is a singular and homogeneous outcome of military socialization and/or military culture and that it is always constructed in opposition to femininity and/or heteronormativity. Titunik's (2008) challenge to narrow definitions of military masculinity went some way to challenge any tendency towards simplistic or pathological definitions by demonstrating that military organizations also revere various personal characteristics traditionally associated with femininity, such as sacrifice, compassion, and cooperation. Thus, militarized masculinities are not constructed purely on the disavowal of all that is feminine or associated with women.

This led to two further developments. The first was a minor interest in female military masculinities (Tasker 2011; Ombati 2015). Tasker used the portrayal of female soldiers in Hollywood films to reconceptualize military masculinity without the male body – influenced by Halberstam's work on female masculinities more generally (Halberstam 1998). Tasker takes Halberstam's conceptualization of non-normative gender and sexuality which is applied to female soldiers who are depicted as occupying a parodic, mimicking or inauthentic military masculinity. In the films *Courage Under Fire* and *GI Jane*, Tasker finds evidence of military masculine space where women are able to perform gender in both conventional and unconventional ways. The actress Demi Moore, for example, labours to shed her 'femininity' by shaving her head and wearing an undershirt traditionally seen as men's attire, in order to be accepted as a legitimate soldier. Moore's character is finally accepted as a legitimate man amongst her male military peers, after she demonstrates her ability to be 'just like the men' in her squad. This work contests the scope of military masculinities by insisting not only on their plurality, but by questioning the very constitution and production of masculinity as a social expression of gender (Ombati 2015).

The other development is found in work examining both military femininity and masculinity, as Dietrich does in her 2012 piece on militarization in Peru, El Salvador, and Colombia. This work, along with that of scholars such Myrttinen (2013), (Parpart and Partridge 2014; Parpart 2015), Maringira (2015), and Stachowitsch (2015), begins to pay attention to internal differences and inequalities amongst men. What these more recent works suggest is that the study of militarized masculinities has expanded considerably and draws on a range of concepts and theories. This is why it is unsurprising that intersectionality has appeared in the literature. Masculinity scholars have looked towards feminist theory for some time now, and in order to understand the complex theoretical terrain of military and militarized masculinities, scholars have turned to 'classic' texts, including that by Crenshaw and other intersectional theorists. As such, it is not surprising that the intersectional 'turn' should now make headway within the study of men, masculinities, and the military.

Critique of recent scholarship employing intersectionality in 'privileged' military contexts

The aforementioned scholarship on diversity and differences in military and militarized settings draws on the concept of diversity in somewhat problematic ways. Intersectionality has not generally been theorized as a 'technology' (as has been previously outlined) – but in the scholarship empirically located in privileged sites or on axes of identity that are assumed to be privileged (i.e. masculinity), I argue that intersectionality figures in a partial and politically incomplete way. Thus, what happens to intersectionality when it is used in militarized empirical spaces? And, subsequently, what happens when intersectionality is discussed in a workshop where black women are mostly absent? What are the ethical and feminist commitments that circulate in these epistemic places? I suggest that when introducing a concept such as intersectionality to the privileged (epistemic and empirical) field of military studies, it is important to reflect on the politics and origins of intersectionality theory in the first instance, and that this can go some way in maintaining or repoliticizing the use of such radical concepts. In this section, I show how intersectionality has been introduced to complicate the theorization and understanding of militarized masculinities, such as in the empirical context of Israel and in conflict zones, and I raise some issues with what this means for a collective analysis of male domination and the power of men in militaries more generally.

If intersectionality can be introduced to sensitize researchers to pay attention to differences and identities as multiple and interconnected, then research interested in examining men's and women's experiences of militarization and the military might be an ideal site. Recent research in military sociology and conflict studies has done just that (Sasson-Levy 2011; 2016; Lomsky-Feder and Sasson-Levy 2015; Myrttinen, Khattab, and Naujoks 2016). While this is a welcome development in many respects, the subfield of militarized masculinities/masculinities in conflict has already undergone considerable contestation in recent times (Kirby and Henry 2012). Kirby and Henry (2012) argue that rethinking masculinity must include an account of masculinity that does not relegate men's violence to pathological or essentialist explanations. This recent work that Kirby and Henry respond to does not take up intersectionality centrally even though it is concerned to challenge simplistic readings of men's practices in conflict and postconflict settings. Several recent pieces of work (partially discussed at the workshop) take up intersectionality in an attempt to problematize gendered, homogenizing tendencies in the work on militarized masculinities. However, this work does not sufficiently acknowledge the history of intersectionality, nor does it provide a structural analysis of inequalities – something of which is central to Crenshaw's original conceptual work. In this way, then, the take-up of intersectionality remains partial and incomplete.

During the Newcastle workshop, Sasson-Levy presented a paper in which she invoked intersectionality and explained how studies of militarized masculinities in the Israeli context have used feminist-inspired theories of difference in order to better understand the differential position and experiences of military personnel. This presentation was based on previously published work which outlines an intersectional approach. What is original is that Sasson-Levy contributes to the introduction (and intervention) of intersectionality into studies of militaries, and as such enables a certain type of analysis which accounts for the multiple positions that military men and women occupy in the specific Israeli context. As Sasson-Levy writes:

> The scholarship on militarized masculinities thus combines intersectionality theory, by examining different groups of men (immigrants, Mizrachim, Ashkenazim, homosexuals), with the inequality regime approach, which looks at various military locations (blue-collar, white-collar, combat). By deconstructing the monolithic conception of militarized masculinity, this research enables us to explore how the military relies on distinct constructions of military masculinity and their interdependence. (Sasson-Levy 2011, 85)

Sasson-Levy focuses on the structuring effects of multiple differences, with an emphasis on gender and class which she argues dictate the limits and opportunities of soldiers within a militarized society and organization. In a stratified social context such as Israel, it is not surprising that scholars have turned to concepts such as intersectionality (and inequality) in order to understand the ways in which differences *matter*. While Sasson-Levy's work acknowledges the roots of intersectionality in black women's lives, and challenges patriarchy and the class system in the Israeli military context, it does not dwell on the idea of intersecting oppressions, nor does it engage substantially with the category of 'race'. In this context, the radical potential of intersectionality to challenge power relations and to make visible the multiple forms of oppression that some individuals experience is sidelined. And while the research is focussed on social differences inside the Israeli military, intersectionality could have been used to focus on the ways in which the specific actions of militarized individuals and the institution contribute to a compounding of oppressions by those subject to the power of the Israeli military in relation to those targeted and racialized as other, such as Palestinians.

A second presentation, also focusing on the Israeli military context, relied upon intersectionality in order to understand the experiences of professional and personal marginalization faced by soldiers of minority ethnic origin. Kachtan's presentation, based on previously published research, reflected many of the social divisions present in Israeli society, with soldiers being distributed into prestigious and powerful positions inside the military organization according to their ethnicity (Grosswirth Kachtan 2015). This practice, it was presented, emanates from competing forms of hegemonic masculinity where processes of ethnicization contribute to hierarchal gender relations (masculinities). Kachtan's presentation suggested that intersectionality had not been used to study differences amongst men in relation to class and ethnicity, although the previously published work begins to theorize the 'intersectional' aspects of masculinity and ethnicity (2015, 16). Kachtan's detailed analysis of the ways in which masculinities are distributed in the gender order challenges the idea of a monolithic military masculinity. The work also draws attention to the intersecting identities that feature within the Israeli military and that give rise to processes of ethnicization, discrimination, and preferential treatment of certain men and, although not specifically focussed upon, racialization. Yet Kachtan's account of marginal military masculinities seems somewhat limited. Kachtan concentrates on two main axes of identity: gender and ethnicity. Although class is somewhat invoked (in regard to social positioning), it is also sometimes integrated with ethnicity. What was not explored in more detail is whether these intersecting differences matter outside of male-dominated institutions, and whether they form the basis for oppression in society more generally. Perhaps what military scholars could do is to link how forms of masculinities relate to femininities within the gender order – after all, fratriarchal relations are relevant to how male domination over women is maintained in patriarchal cultures.[1]

While the attention to multiple or intersectional differences seems to be an important development in studies of Israeli society, it is curious how little of the scholarship provides a rationale for why intersectionality is the most appropriate conceptual frame for understanding military men's experiences (of marginality or privilege). Why should the concept of intersectionality (and therefore intersecting oppressions) be used to study marginality within such a powerful and exclusive institution as the military? In both presentations and the previous or subsequent published work there is only the briefest of connections made to black feminist thought and to some of the history and context of intersectionality. Despite intersectionality sensitizing the researchers to differences within gender groups and experiences of marginality, the invisibilization of poor, 'racialized' women inside and outside of the military is not attended to in any meaningful way. What of the Palestinian gendered subjects who remain eclipsed in these accounts of gender marginality? Thus, how is it that Israeli female soldiers or Israeli 'ethnic' soldiers are only acknowledged to be positioned on the 'margins' within their militaries, but not at the centre, or in privileged ways in relation to 'other' women civilians?

These presentations and articles are reflective of the broader trend in how intersectionality is used. In a recent article, Feder-Lomsky and Sasson-Levy invoke the concept of intersectionality (2015). In this piece, there are no explicit references to the work of US Black feminists or to Crenshaw herself. This omission is not particularly surprising as it might be that intersectionality has become so ubiquitous and mainstreamed in academic research that it has begun to take on a *quotidian* feel. Has intersectionality come so far that it has left its black mothers behind? Has it been so successfully co-opted into FCMS that there is no longer a requirement to remember and acknowledge its own political heritage? I suggest that recent work on intersectionality could do so much more and that future work should see a return to the origins of the concept, not as a disciplinary requirement but as a way of moving across epistemic time and space in order to engage in a transversal politics (Yuval-Davis 1997). It could, for example, make visible the hierarchical ways in which gender is manifest in a militarized society, and acknowledge the history of the concept of intersectionality without giving up the possibility to use intersectionality in politically challenging ways.

Interestingly, a similar trend is noticeable in some work on men and vulnerability in conflict affected regions (Myrttinen, Khattab, and Naujoks 2016). This work uses intersectionality rather instrumentally, and more as a sensitizing concept in the context of the highly politicized space of the humanitarian. It draws attention, once again, to the idea that militarized masculinities are not created equally, and that many men experience marginalization and a loss of power in the face of hegemonic forms of power. In another presentation, this time interested in militarized masculinities in conflict contexts, intersectionality is invoked in order to better understand men's (this time contradictory) experiences of war (see Myrttinen, Khattab, and Naujoks 2016). In this emerging field of masculinity studies is an interest in men, masculinity, and vulnerability in conflict contexts. Myrttinen et al. highlight the ways in which men in militarized contexts may be made marginal and even vulnerable in times of war, where masculinities are suddenly redesigned and reordered.

Drawing on the concept of 'thwarted' masculinities, Myrttinen, Khattab, and Naujoks (2016) argue that the pressure for men to conform and perform to hegemonic ideals of masculinity can be a source of frustration for men living in warzones. Men may be subject to militarization and martial values in the wake of not being able to exercise hegemonic power and agency and not being able to attain the 'dividends' that male power promises (Connell 1995). However, it is not only thwarted masculinities that illustrate the marginal experiences of some men, but also the vulnerabilities that men experience as a result of societal expectations. Myrttinen et al. use the example of taxi drivers in Sierra Leone and Liberia, who are often assumed to be ex-combatants and therefore treated as militarized men – that is, men who deserve to be doled out forms of violent 'revenge' (Myrttinen, Khattab, and Naujoks 2016, 8). These men, they reveal, are often marginalized because of their current and poor economic positioning. Without significant economic power, ex-combatants and poor men in conflict zones can be at risk of violence and social marginalization. Furthermore, challenging the idea that women are only vulnerable and men only perpetrators/predators, the article focusses on the ways in which gender relations subject some men to a stigmatized or compromised social position. Another example they draw upon is that of male victims of sexual violence (Myrttinen, Khattab, and Naujoks 2016: 10). Here they suggest that along with thwarted masculinity, and vulnerable and stigmatized positionalities, men in conflict settings do not uniformly benefit from patriarchal structures and the gender order. Victims of sexual violence are often invisible, or fear the repercussions for social perceptions of their 'compromised' maleness. And, as such, Myrttinen et al.'s work challenges the idea of military masculinities as resulting in wholesale power, especially when examining the ways in which men face the risk of violence unevenly within conflict and postconflict societies.

When seeking to look at the margins of military masculinities, it is not surprising that scholars seek out concepts and theories which provide a complex picture and which permit making linkages and seeing points of intersection and even compoundment. In this section I have argued that while intersectionality can sensitize researchers to the complexity of militarized masculinities and the marginal position of some men, especially in conflict zones, it does not go far enough in challenging patriarchal power relations that persist. This is because masculinity is not only constructed in relation to other masculinities. And, consequently, militarized masculinities are not constructed only in relation to one another. A more theoretical and politically 'authentic' account of masculinity must return in some way to the system in which militarized masculinities function – that of the gender order or regime (Connell 1995). If the main aim of the gender order or patriarchy is domination of women, then a logical extension of these analyses should be to question in what ways these new conceptualizations and empirical investigations into multiplicity challenge existing gender relations. How is the hegemony of men, in the end, contested (Hearn 2004)?

Intersectional sensitivities in FCMS: learning from Global South peacekeepers

Perhaps the process of sensitization to intersectionality (and its traditional and non-traditional uses) stems also from my own position as a Black woman doing work on female militarized personnel (Henry 2012). Similarly, in recent research on the everyday lives and identities of militarized peacekeepers, I have argued that peacekeepers are not all positioned equally within the peacekeeping economy (Henry 2015). In particular, in a study of peacekeepers in the United Nations (UN) peacekeeping operation in Liberia (UNMIL) in 2012–2013, I found that there are considerable differences between and amongst male peacekeepers, for example from West Africa, and between and amongst female peacekeepers, as in the case of those from South Asia (Henry 2015).

In this research, male peacekeepers from the Global South are often particularly conscious about their image and reputation within the peacekeeping space. When visiting the Nigerian Battalion stationed outside of Monrovia, I was told repeatedly by the commander that 'his men were not involved in sexual exploitation and abuse' and that this was a result of 'strict disciplinary regimes' instituted by the leaders and 'top brass'. This statement was repeated (at least three times) throughout the interview, despite the fact that I had made clear that the objective was to research the everyday experiences of peacekeepers and their positive contributions to the local communities. Nigerian peacekeepers portrayed themselves as hard-working and upstanding men, who prided themselves on a professional and disciplined working environment. By not interacting with local people other than under very regulated conditions, Nigerian peacekeepers refashioned themselves under a more disciplined and 'clean' masculinity. Their accounts were continually and implicitly comparative. The commander recounted how 'his men' were highly trained and professional, and he facilitated a further set of observations and interviews with a group of Nigerian peacekeepers giving physics lessons in a local high school in Monrovia. A central concern to Nigerian male (and the few female) peacekeepers was to improve their reputation amongst locals and internationals, as they believed their conduct and image from previous missions were less than commendable (see also Higate and Henry 2009). Similarly, male military peacekeepers from Ghana shared with me their own versions of their distinctive masculine identities, which they felt were in significant contrast to those of local Liberian men. They repeatedly told me that they believed they had a very different 'African' culture to Liberians and, as such, saw themselves as ideal peacekeepers who were able to transfer 'positive' messages and ideas to local communities. One of the reasons for their insistence on distinctiveness from Liberians was that they too had an investment in presenting themselves *not* as marginalized subjects of the Global South – but as peacekeepers from an elevated and experienced position. Their accounts emphasized differences in many ways, but they actively worked to position themselves *not* at the geopolitical margins as they might casually be placed by peacekeepers from the Global North, or the UN community more generally, but at the centre. Their position as 'marginal' men was continuously disavowed, and as such this research finding suggests that not all those who might be positioned in intersectionally different ways are without power, or without a desire to be seen as powerful. What I am arguing here is that there is a complex relationship between identity, positionality, and power, and this is especially brought out in studies of marginal military men. Intersectionality as a concept can sensitize researchers to the fact that not all 'margins' are equally placed in the gender order, nor are all men positioned similarily in the global order. And the axes of difference that contribute to oppression may individually provide an opportunity for the exercise of hegemonic power. In this way, using intersectionality to help in the analysis of women's and men's marginalization or vulnerability in a given context does not always provide a full picture of the nature of power more broadly speaking.

A similar pattern can be found when thinking about female peacekeepers from the Global South. In the same research study as above, female peacekeepers from the Philippines, Ghana, Nepal, and India articulated their own elevated class position vis-à-vis local women by asserting their distinct culture. Indian women peacekeepers, for example, found local women to be sexually 'promiscuous' because of their non-gender-segregated cultural practices (Henry 2015; see also Henry 2012). These female peacekeepers did not see themselves as oppressed along multiple axes of difference. Instead, these women demonstrated consistently how their privilege and positions of power in their home societies enabled them to be deployed in the first place. For example, all four national groups shared that their presence was made possible by the easily and cheaply available labour of 'poor' women in their home countries. The global division of labour provided an opportunity for these marginalized and militarized peacekeepers to maintain various forms of power, privilege, and dividends. That is, they were able to leave their families and children at home because of the availability of poor female labourers who provide domestic and social reproductive labour while they work abroad. Here, deploying an intersectional lens would better be used to highlight the maintenance of class and/or caste benefits, rather than to stress the relative weight of multiple differences. In fact, the idea of interlocking privileges might be particularly apt.

A final example comes from the ways in which Indian female peacekeepers adopted a form of female militarized masculinity. While this form of masculinity demonstrated their difference from traditional emphasized forms, it enabled women to maintain themselves in positions of relative power within their national contexts. Indian women peacekeepers were highly skilled and trained in martial arts and advanced weapons use (see also Henry 2012, 2015; Pruitt 2016). They adopted *excessive* martial military identities and garnered significant salaries as a result (at least in comparison to those opting for national duty only). In doing so, these women attempted to position themselves in hegemonic ways in relation to local women, and to challenge forms of hegemonic masculinity within their national militaries. The intersections of difference for them did not result in compounding oppressions, but rather they actively benefitted from the different forms of capital that they amassed through their own privileged backgrounds (Henry 2015).

An intersectional sensitivity to the unequal positioning of peacekeepers from the Global South in peacekeeping economies provides an opportunity to acknowledge the structural inequalities that feature in global and militarized peacekeeping. Clearly, not all peacekeepers are created equally (see Higate and Henry 2009; Henry 2012, 2015). I have argued that while intersectionality can sensitize us to differences amongst male and female military personnel, it does not provide scholars with sufficient tools to challenge the hegemonic position of men (or some women) in a variety of national military contexts. Instead, scholars need to pay attention to the flip side of the intersectional coin – that of privileges, benefits, and power gains maintained and crystallized through either the power of the military or patriarchy itself.

Conclusion: where are the women?

In very recent work, Crenshaw takes up intersectional challenges and critiques a tendency within critical race theory (CRT) to use intersectionality in order to illustrate the problematic focus on *male* victims of racialized violence, as is evident in social media campaigns such as *Black Lives Matter* and slogans such as 'I Can't Breathe' used in a variety of activist contexts (Enloe 1989). Crenshaw has taken up new research to return to poor black women who are also victims of police/state violence in the US through the campaign 'Say Her Name' – which uses intersectionality to examine women's invisibility in larger 'post-post racial' narratives (Crenshaw et al. 2015). This work has led me to think carefully about how we deploy radical concepts like intersectionality within a field of study that itself perpetuates racial hierarchies (by the low employment of black and ethnic minority scholars in IR/CMS/FCMS), and in the ongoing whiteness of syllabi concerned with gender issues in militarized contexts.

Intersectionality is not wisely used when it is only deployed to examine difference. Instead, intersectionality can help the study of military masculinity and militarized masculinities by reminding us of what is lost when we study gender and masculinities without women and without feminist inspiration. As Enloe famously asked so long ago, where are the women? I would add, where are the poor black women in the military? We know many black women are employed within the US military in much larger numbers than is generally represented in the literature analysing intersectionality and the military. If my own experiences of being marginalized, my particular standpoint, can enable me to see a variety of oppressions, silences, and absences in the literature and in the practice of academia – then perhaps the next step is for scholars to take seriously intersectional research. What is desperately needed in FCMS is a return to thinking not only about differences, but about the differences that result in multiple and intersecting oppressions for those who are already marginalized by 'race', class, and gender (to start with). And, for the meantime, that is not military men.

Note

1. This point is taken up in more depth by Sasson-Levy (2011), but suprisingly not so by Higate (2012).

Acknowledgements

Thanks to a number of individuals who provided feedback to me on versions of this paper, including faculty at the Gender Institute, LSE and Alexandra Hyde, Harriet Gray, Victoria

Basham, Sarah Bulmer, Catherine Baker, Melanie Richter-Monpetit, Paul Amar, and Henri Myrttinen; and especially Amanda Chisholm and Joanna Tidy. As always, I am indebted to those scholars whose work continually inspires: Cynthia Enloe and Kimberley Crenshaw.

Disclosure statement

No potential conflict of interest was reported by the author.

References

Ackerly, B., and J. True 2008. An intersectional analysis of international relations: Recasting the discipline. *Politics & Gender* 4, no. 1: 156–73. doi:10.1017/S1743923X08000081

Ackerly, B.A., M. Stern, and J. True eds. 2006. *Feminist methodologies for international relations*. Cambridge: Cambridge University Press.

Alexander, M.J., and C.T. Mohanty 1997. *Feminist genealogies, colonial legacies, democratic futures*. New York, NY: Routledge.

Amar, P. 2011. Middle east masculinity studies discourses of "men in crisis", industries of gender in revolution. *Journal of Middle East Women's Studies* 7, no. 3: 36–70. doi:10.2979/jmiddeastwomstud.7.3.36

Amar, P. 2013. *The Security Archipelago: Human-security States, sexuality politics, and the end of neoliberalism*. Durham: Duke University Press.

Anthias, F., and N. Yuval-Davis 1992. *Racialized boundaries: Race, nation, gender, colour and class and the anti-racist struggle*. London: Routledge.

Anzaldúa, G. 1987. *Borderlands: The new mestiza = la frontera Frontera*. 1st ed. San Francisco, CA: Aunt Lute Books.

Atherton, S. 2014. The geographies of military inculcation and domesticity: Reconceptualising masculinities at home, Gorman-Murray, A and Hopkins, P (Eds): Masculinities and Place, Farnham: Ashgate, 143-257.

Baaz, M.E. and Stern, M., 2009. Why do soldiers rape? masculinity, violence, and sexuality in the armed forces in the Congo (DRC). *International Studies Quarterly* 53, no. 2: 495–518. doi:10.1111/isqu.2009.53.issue-2

Baaz, M., and M. Stern 2013. Sexual violence as a weapon of war? Perceptions, prescriptions, problems in the Congo and beyond, London: Zed Press.

Belkin, A. 2012. *Bring me men: Military masculinity and the benign façade of American empire, 1898-2001*. London: Columbia University Press.

Bilge, S. 2013. Intersectionality undone. *Du Bois Review: Social Science Research on Race* 10, no. 02: 405–24. doi:10.1017/S1742058X13000283

Brah, A., and A. Phoenix 2004. Ain't i a woman? revisiting intersectionality. *Journal of International Women's Studies* 5, no. 3: 75–86.

Carbado, D.W. 2013. Colorblind intersectionality. *Signs: Journal of Women in Culture and Society* 38, no. 4: 811–45. doi:10.1086/669666

Cho, S., K.W. Crenshaw, and L. McCall 2013. Toward a field of intersectionality studies: Theory, applications, and praxis. *Signs: Journal of Women in Culture and Society* 38, no. 4: 785–810. doi:10.1086/669608

Cockburn, C. 2010. Gender relations as causal in militarization and war. *International Feminist Journal of Politics* 12, no. 2: 139–57. doi:10.1080/14616741003665169

Collins, P.H. 1986. Learning from the outsider within: The sociological significance of Black feminist thought. *Social Problems* 33, no. 6: s14–s32. doi:10.2307/800672

Collins, P.H. 1989. The social construction of black feminist thought. *Signs: Journal of Women in Culture and Society* 14, no. 4: 745–73. doi:10.1086/494543

Collins, P.H. 2000. *Black feminist thought: Knowledge, consciousness, and the politics of empowerment*. 2nd ed. New York, NY: Routledge.

Collins, P.H., and S. Bilge 2016. *Intersectionality.* Cambridge: John Wiley and Sons.

Connell, R.W. 1987. *Gender and power.* Sydney: Allen and Unwin.

Connell, R.W. 1995. *Masculinities.* Cambridge, UK: Polity Press.

Connell, R.W., and J.W. Messerschmidt 2005. Hegemonic masculinity rethinking the concept. *Gender & Society* 19, no. 6: 829–59. doi:10.1177/0891243205278639

Conway, D. 2012. *Masculinities, militarisation and the End Conscription campaign: War resistance in apartheid South Africa.* Manchester: Manchester University Press.

Crenshaw, K. 1989. Demarginalizing the intersection of race and sex: A black feminist critique of antidiscrimination doctrine, feminist theory and antiracist politics. *University of Chicago Legal Forum* 1989.

Crenshaw, K. 1991. Mapping the margins: Intersectionality, identity politics, and violence against women of color. *Stanford Law Review* 43, no. 6: 1241–99. doi:10.2307/1229039

Crenshaw, K., A.J. Ritchie, R. Anspach, R. Gilmer, and L. Harris 2015. *Say her name: Resisting police brutality against black women* New York: African American Policy Forum.

Davis, K. 2008. Intersectionality as buzzword: A sociology of science perspective on what makes a feminist theory successful. *Feminist Theory* 9, no. 1: 67–85. doi:10.1177/1464700108086364

de Silva, J. 2014. Valour, violence and the ethics of struggle: Constructing militant masculinities in Sri Lanka. *South Asian History and Culture* 5, no. 4: 438–56. doi:10.1080/19472498.2014.936204

Dietrich Ortega, L.M. 2012. Looking beyond violent militarized masculinities: Guerrilla gender regimes in Latin America. *International Feminist Journal of Politics* 14, no. 4: 489–507. doi:10.1080/14616742.2012.726094

Dudink, S., K. Hagemann, and J. Tosh eds. 2004. *Masculinities in politics and war: Gendering modern history.* Manchester, UK: Manchester University Press.

Duncanson, C. 2009. Forces for good? Narratives of military masculinity in peacekeeping operations. *International Feminist Journal of Politics* 11, no. 1: 63–80. doi:10.1080/14616740802567808

Duncanson, C. 2013. *Forces for good?: Military masculinities and peacebuilding in Afghanistan and Iraq.* London: Springer.

Duncanson, C. 2015. Hegemonic masculinity and the possibility of change in gender relations. *Men and Masculinities* 18, no. 2: 231–48. doi:10.1177/1097184X15584912

Enloe, C 1983. *Does khaki become you? the militarization of women's lives,* Boston: Southend Press.

Enloe, C. 1989. *Bananas, beaches and bases,* London: Pandora Press.

Enloe, C. 1994. *Gender makes the world go round.* In Wells, D (Ed.) Getting there: The movement toward gender equality, New York: Carroll and Graf Publishers/Richard Galllen Publishers Inc., 166–185.

Enloe, C. 2000. *Maneuvers: the international politics of militarizing women's lives* Berkeley: University of California Press.

Enloe, C. 2002. *Masculinity as a Foreign Policy Issue,* in Hawthorne, S. and Winter, B. (Eds) September 11, 2001: Feminist Perspectives, Melbourne: Spinifex Press, 284–289.

Enloe, C., 2006. Macho, macho military. *The Nation,* March 6.

Falcón, S.M., and J.C. Nash 2015. Shifting analytics and linking theories: A conversation about the "meaning-making" of intersectionality and transnational feminism. *Women's Studies International Forum* 50: 1–10.doi:10.1016/j.wsif.2015.02.010

Fernandes, L. 2015. Intersectionality and disciplinarity: Reflections from an international perspective. *New Political Science* 37, no. 4: 643–48. doi:10.1080/07393148.2015.1089046

Grewal, I., and C. Kaplan 1994. *Scattered hegemonies: Postmodernity and transnational feminist practices.* Minneapolis: University of Minnesota Press.

Grosswirth Kachtan, D. 2015. "Acting Ethnic"—Performance of ethnicity and the process of ethnicization. *Ethnicities* 0, no. 0: 1–20.

Halberstam, J. 1998. *Female masculinity.* Durham: Duke University Press.

Hancock, A.-M. 2007. When multiplication doesn't equal quick addition: Examining intersectionality as a research paradigm. *Perspectives on Politics* 5, no. 1: 63–79. doi:10.1017/S1537592707070065

Hancock, A.-M. 2016. *Intersectionality: An intellectual history.* Oxford: Oxford University Press.

Haraway, D. 1988. Situated knowledges: The science question in feminism and the privilege of partial perspective. *Feminist Studies* 14, no. 3: 575–99. doi:10.2307/3178066

Harding, S. 1986. The instability of the analytical categories of feminist theory. *Signs: Journal of Women in Culture and Society* 11, no. 4: 645–64. doi:10.1086/494270

Hartsock, N.C. 1983. The feminist standpoint: Developing the ground for a specifically feminist historical materialism. In Harding, S. (Ed) *Discovering reality*, 283–310. Springer Netherlands.

Hearn, J. 2004. From hegemonic masculinity to the hegemony of men. *Feminist Theory* 5, no. 1: 49–72. doi:10.1177/1464700104040813

Henry, M. 2012. Peacexploitation? Interrogating labor hierarchies and global sisterhood among Indian and Uruguayan female peacekeepers. *Globalizations* 9, no. 1: 15–33. doi:10.1080/14747731.2012.627716

Henry, M. 2015. Parades, Parties and Pests: Contradictions of Everyday Life in Peacekeeping Economies. *Journal of Intervention and Statebuilding* 9, no. 3: 372–90. doi:10.1080/17502977.2015.1070021

Higate, P. ed. 2003. *Military masculinities: Identity and the state*. London: Praeger Publishers.

Higate, P. 2012. Drinking vodka from the Butt-Crack: Men, masculinities and fratriarchy in the private militarized security company. *International Feminist Journal of Politics* 14, no. 4: 450–69. doi:10.1080/14616742.2012.726092

Higate, P., and M. Henry 2009. *Insecure spaces: Peacekeeping, power and performance in Kosovo, Liberia and Haiti*, London.

hooks, B. 1984. *Feminist theory: From margin to center*. Boston, MA: South End Press.

Jordan-Zachery, J. 2013. Now you see me, now you don't: My political fight against the invisibility/erasure of black women in intersectionality research. *Politics, Groups, and Identities* 1, no. 1: 101–09. doi:10.1080/21565503.2012.760314

Kirby, P., and M. Henry 2012. Rethinking masculinity and practices of violence in conflict settings. *International Feminist Journal of Politics* 14, no. 4: 445–49. doi:10.1080/14616742.2012.726091

Kronsell, A., and E. Svedberg eds. 2012. *Making gender, making war: Violence, military and peacekeeping practices*. New York, NY: Routledge.

Lewis, G. 2009. *Celebrating intersectionality? Debates on a multi-faceted concept in gender studies: Themes from a conference European Journal of Women's Studies*, 16, no. 3: 203–210.

Lewis, G. 2013. Unsafe travel: Experiencing intersectionality and feminist displacements. *Signs: Journal of Women in Culture and Society* 38, no. 4: 869–92. doi:10.1086/669609

Lomsky-Feder, E., and O. Sasson-Levy 2015. Serving the army as secretaries: Intersectionality, multi-level contract and subjective experience of citizenship. *The British Journal of Sociology* 66, no. 1: 173–92. doi:10.1111/1468-4446.12102

Lomsky-Feder, E., and T. Rapoport 2003. Juggling models of masculinity: russian-jewish immigrants in the israeli army, *Sociological Inquiry*, 73, no.1: 114–137.

Lorde, A. 1984. *Sister outsider: Essays and speeches*. Trumansburg, NY: Crossing Press.

Lugones, M. and Spelman, E. 1983. Have we got a theory for you: Feminist Theory, cultural imperialism and the demand for the "woman's voice", Hypatia 1: 573–581

Maringira, G. 2015. Militarised minds: The lives of ex-combatants in South Africa. *Sociology* 49, no. 1: 72–87. doi:10.1177/0038038514523698

Masters, C. 2005. Bodies of technology: Cyborg soldiers and militarized masculinities. *International Feminist Journal of Politics* 7, no. 1: 112–32. doi:10.1080/1461674042000324718

McCall, L. 2005. The complexity of intersectionality. *Signs: Journal of Women in Culture and Society* 30, no. 3: 1771–800. doi:10.1086/426800

Moraga, C.E., and G. Anzaldúa 1983. *This bridge called my back: Writings by radical women of color*. 2nd ed. New York, NY: Kitchen Table.

Murib, Z., and J. Soss 2015. Intersectionality as an assembly of analytic practices: Subjects, relations and situated comparisons. *New Political Science* 37, no. 4: 649–56. doi:10.1080/07393148.2015.1089047

Myrttinen, H. 2013. Phantom Menaces: The Politics of Rumour, Securitisation and Masculine Identities in the Shadows of the Ninjas. *The Asia Pacific Journal of Anthropology* 14, no. 5: 471–85. doi:10.1080/14442213.2013.821154

Myrttinen, H., L. Khattab, and J. Naujoks 2016. Re-thinking hegemonic masculinities in conflict-affected contexts. *Critical Military Studies* 1–17. doi:10.1080/23337486.2016.1262658

Nash, J.C. 2016. Feminist originalism: Intersectionality and the politics of reading. *Feminist Theory* 17, no. 1: 3–20. doi:10.1177/1464700115620864

Ombati, M. 2015. Feminine masculinities in the military: The case of female combatants in the Kenya Defence Forces' operation in Somalia. *African Security Review* 24, no. 4: 403–13. doi:10.1080/10246029.2015.1099339

Parpart, J., and K. Partridge 2014. *Soldiering on: Pushing militarised masculinities into new territory*, in Evans, M; Hemmings, C; Henry, M; Johnstone, H; Madhok, S; Plomien, A; and Wearing, S (Eds), The SAGE handbook of feminist theory, London: Sage, 550-565.

Parpart, J.L. 2015. Militarized masculinities, heroes and gender inequality during and after the nationalist struggle in Zimbabwe. *NORMA* 10, no. 3–4: 312–25. doi:10.1080/18902138.2015.1110434

Pruitt, L. 2016. *The women in blue helmets: gender, policing, and the un's first all-female peace-keeping unit*, Berkeley: University of California Press.

Rommel, C. 2016. Troublesome thugs or respectable rebels? class, martyrdom and Cairo's revolutionary ultras. *Middle East-Topics & Arguments* 6: 33–42.

Sasson-Levy, O. 2011. Research on gender and the military in Israel: From a gendered organization to inequality regimes. *Israel Studies Review* 26, no. 2: 73–98. doi:10.3167/isr.2011.260205

Sasson-Levy, O. 2016. Women's memories of soldiering: An intersectionality perspective. *Gendered Wars, Gendered Memories: Feminist Conversations on War, Genocide and Political Violence* Abingdon, Oxford: Routledge,: 109-120.

Smith, D.E. 1987. *The everyday world as problematic: A feminist sociology.* Toronto: University of Toronto Press.

Stachowitsch, S. 2015. The reconstruction of masculinities in global politics: Gendering strategies in the field of private security. *Men and Masculinities* 18, no. 3: 363–86. doi:10.1177/1097184X14551205

Sylvester, C. 2013. *War as experience: Contributions from international relations and feminist analysis.* Milton Park: Routledge.

Tasker, Y. 2011. *Soldiers' Stories: Military Women in Cinema and Television since World War II.* Durham: Duke University Press.

Tidy, J. 2016. The gender politics of "Ground Truth" in the military dissent movement: The power and limits of authenticity claims regarding war. *International Political Sociology* 10, no. 2: 99–114. doi:10.1093/ips/olw003

Titunik, R.F. 2008. The myth of the macho military. *Polity* 40, no. 2: 137–63. doi:10.1057/palgrave.polity.2300090

Tomlinson, B. 2013. Colonizing intersectionality: Replicating racial hierarchy in feminist academic arguments. *Social Identities* 19, no. 2: 254–72. doi:10.1080/13504630.2013.789613

Whitworth, S. 2004. *Men, militarism, and UN peacekeeping: A gendered analysis.* Boulder, Colorado: Lynne Rienner Publishers.

Wibben, A.T.R. ed. 2016. *Researching war: Feminist methods, ethics and politics.* London: Routledge.

Yuval-Davis, N. 1997. Women, citizenship and difference. *Feminist Review* 57, no. 1: 4–27. doi:10.1080/014177897339632

Zalewski, M., and J. Parpart eds. 1998. *The "Man" question in international relations.* University of Michigan: Westview Press.

Zalewski, M., and J. Parpart 2008. Rethinking the man question: Sex, gender and violence in international relations, London: Zed Books: 1-20.

Zarkov, D. 2011. Exposures and invisibilities: Media, masculinities and the narratives of wars in an intersectional perspective in Lutz, H.; Herrera, MT Vivar; Supik, L (Eds): *Framing Intersectionality*: Debates on a multi-faceted Concept in Gender Studies, 105-120.

What's the problem with the concept of military masculinities?

Marysia Zalewski

ABSTRACT

This think piece queries the value of the concept of military masculinities. This overly familiar and comfortable concept is perhaps falling short of its intended ambitions. Masculinized and militarized violence is rampant and no amount of 'adding women' (or other 'others') seems to make a difference. This begs the question of how much work we imagine concepts can do, as well as how much control we think we have over them.

Military masculinity is … positioned as a status that, by definition, indicates the truth about who and what a man is. (Belkin 2012, 10)

… particular constructions of masculinity depend on militarism and militarism depends on those constructions of masculinity. (Duncanson 2013, 19)

Masculine identity is born in the renunciation of the feminine. (Kimmel, quoted in Belkin 2012, 26)

My point of departure in this 'think-piece' is the idea that the concept of military masculinities has become overly familiar and 'comfortable', at least within feminist scholarship, and that this 'cosiness' is problematic. Familiarity and comfort are not easily measurable things, but there was clearly a sense at the workshop at which this piece originated[1] that there was 'something about' military masculinities that invited critical re-investigation. It is a concept that has found a secure place in feminist political and scholarly arsenals on militarization, not least given its rich empirical exposé of the political and gendered power the masculinized military body produces – so what might be wrong with it now?

I think part of the reason we, as feminist/critical scholars, are prompted to ask this kind of question is because we sense that the critical work expected of a particular concept is failing to achieve in some way. Or, indeed, potentially working against feminist-inspired expectations and hopes. A helpful way to start thinking about this is to consider what some of these expectations might have been. What do or did feminists and critical scholars really expect to achieve through the successful infiltration and deployment of the idea of military masculinities? Less violent soldiering? Probably. Less frequent wars? Possibly. Less aggressive governments? Perhaps. And of course so much more and other than any of these more obvious sites, it is a concept which is integrally connected to a wide range of feminist hopes and ambitions.

Though it is tempting at this point to offer a definition of military masculinities to proceed with the discussion, my suspicion is that precision around meaning is not the most immediate issue at stake here – though the opening quotations provide helpful prompts. Rather, the increasing frustrations with the concept, which are importantly linked to its 'easy' uptake by hegemonic governance institutions, and associated paradoxical concerns that military masculinities might doing more harm than good, invite deeper questioning about the work of a concept itself. Concepts are simply invented to provide a vocabulary – literal and epistemic – to help us in political, intellectual, and educative agendas, specifically through the reconceptualization of allegedly natural or irrelevant relationship (between gender and unequal pay for example) as political and unfair. But do concepts run out of steam or become unusable or indeed co-opted? And can concepts feasibly perform the same functions over time given changes, sometimes radical, in political, social, and cultural landscapes? How much control do we have over concepts and their use and meanings?

Kathy Davis offers an interesting sociological analysis of the ways some concepts gain popular acceptance and traction and are taken up with some ease by a range of users such as academics and policymakers (2008). Key features for these popular concepts include being appealing to both generalists and specialists, particularly if they appear to be readily understandable and (relatively) easily applied. They also typically have the capacity to invite a wide range of new empirical and theoretical enquiries. The concept of military masculinities could fit fairly easily into this pattern, perhaps especially in earlier iterations of it. The drill sergeant's traditional homophobic and misogynist taunts to get new recruits into (manly) shape lend themselves to obvious reconfiguration using lessons learned through the concept of military masculinities. Educating military personnel, especially in post-conflict zones, to perform more 'acceptable' masculine behaviours is central to many a 'gender advisor's' toolkit. But concepts are not static things and are only faintly secured to scholars' and others' control of their use and meaning.

Despite the nuances and complexities that critical academic scholarship introduces into theorization of concepts, less-opaque versions characteristically draw and hold popular interest. Paying attention to some of the less nuanced versions of military masculinities, Aaron Belkin has richly illustrated the ways in which the strong evidence of varying and contradictory manifestations of military masculinities in practice have been persistently flattened into a consistent form through some of the scholarly literatures (2012, 17) suggestive of the potential for unhelpful implementation, at least from critical perspectives. A key move or perhaps 'complication' which has additionally fuelled concerns about the work of the concept is the decreasing significance of the male body in military action or units. What does the concept of military masculinities look like when removed from the male body? The connection between militarized bodies and men has clearly become less reliable given the increasing presence of female soldiers.[2] The prior undoubtedness and strength of the association between 'male military bodies' and classic imaginaries of male muscularity – aggressiveness, strength, heroism, and 'manly' behaviours, epitomized in the idealized figure of the 'military man' – can no longer hold. Soldiering can be as well (or as badly) carried out by a range of gendered and 'othered' bodies, casting into doubt the firm connections between manhood and militarism. Is this something we should be concerned about, especially given suspicions that the concept may no longer serve some of its feminist purposes?

A photo I have sometimes shown in classes on gender, masculinity, and war is one that depicts the ending of the Belsan school siege in September 2004. Armed separatists (mostly Chechen) invaded School Number One in the Russian town of Beslan, taking 1100 people hostage (including 777 children). The siege ended after three days when Russian military forces stormed the building with tanks and incendiary rockets. At least 385 people were killed, including 186 children.

The photo (accessible at http://edition.cnn.com/2013/09/09/world/europe/beslan-school-siege-fast-facts/index.html, Photo number 5) captures some of the chaos and panic that must have saturated the three days of the siege, but most violently and terrifyingly at its bloody end. It shows a tangled mass of people: two women (presumably teachers) in bloodstained summer dresses, and five or six soldiers in military fatigues, two with rifles ready to fire. A seemingly faultless gender-infused representation of rescuers and rescued, it certainly looks like the epitome of militarized masculinity in action – though it is not possible to tell if all the soldiers are (all) male. I ask students whether it matters if the soldiers are men or women. Does the worth of the concept of militarized masculinity require that those who practise it, or (literally) embody it, be men? If it doesn't, does this really evacuate the worth of the term 'military masculinities' along with its saturation in all that the conventional binary offers? How do the gendered bodies matter in this context?

Let's suppose one of these soldiers is a woman. We might reasonably assume that the female soldier is as good as or as bad as any of the other soldiers given she must have achieved the required qualifications. This simply means she can fight, kill, and defend as well (or as badly) as any other soldier, or, more typically, carry out the banal work of everyday soldiering.[3] So, in a very practical sense in the situation depicted in the photo, it doesn't matter that one of these soldiers might be a woman. Does that mean that the concept of 'militarized masculinities' has *already* been removed from the male body? Or perhaps it was never attached at all if so easily dislodged? Or perhaps this is the *wrong* question to ask, especially as it so firmly positions gender/sex in the site of the binary corporeal form, a fleshly binary which has so convincingly been demonstrated by decades of feminist and critical scholarship as inadequate. Let's backtrack a little to think more about that which is so deeply at the core of why any of this matters: violence.

Violence

Militaries most surely have violence at their heart; yet, as many feminist and critical scholars have shown, this violence persistently masquerades as something 'other' through its sanctioning by the state. Buried in this authoritative frame is a quagmire of hidden violence – state violence itself, gender/sex violence, the violence of colonialism and racial brutality. Paradoxically, the presence of these contradictions makes militaries a significant maker of gender (and other) boundaries, but also extremely vulnerable to their exposure given the colossal amount of work needed to maintain the web of illusions which create an aura of distance from violence and the associated constitutive work of gender. In part this is why the concept of military masculinities has seemingly proved so useful, as it seemed to provide some essential epistemological and political tools to expose these barely visible relationships.

Terrell Carver's conversation with Aaron Belkin is useful to briefly invoke here, given their discussion of the relationship between militarized masculinities and the erasure of violence (2012). Though the concept of military masculinities might be credited with making the violence at the heart of the military more legible, Carver suspects that the violence has simply become *better erased*. I wonder if this is something to do with a generic familiarity and comfort (certainly in western cultures) with the idea of masculinity *as* a concept, though in practice this morphs into something more like 'social role'. Popular TV and radio shows, magazine articles, blog sites, and social media are awash with pop-psych discussions of the work of masculinity, sometimes explicitly using the concept, sometimes not.[4] Moreover, competing imaginaries of masculinity consistently emerge, for example in popular representations of 'terrorists' and 'western (civilized) leaders'; or at least ideas about masculinities are working to impart particular stories about terrorism through these representations. In general, publics as well as scholars appear to have become very comfortable with the concept of masculinity in all its intersectional permutations. Has the concept become so comfortable that its capacities to expose violence have morphed into capacities to erase violence?

Despite the complexities, nuances, and ephemerality of the connections between gender and bodies, I think there remains a visceral attachment to the suturing of gender (as binary form) to corporeality, to bodies, certainly in the scholarly literature and the typical ways these get taken up by hegemonic institutions. I think this is apparent in the sense of destabilization when there is a clear exposure of its construction, that actually the central cultural 'identifiers' of gender don't matter, at least in the context of hegemonic military missions. The ephemerality of corporeal attachment materializes as significantly disturbing given the boundary work of militarized masculinities has become such a convincing route through which to expose violence. This attachment and difficulty of separating the corporeal binary of gender reveals itself even in the critically inspired conversation between Belkin and Carver through the fairly regular use of gendered parentheses in their discussion. Here are some examples – 'the current rival of (men's) sports' (563); 'the "womenandchildren"' 'he (or a sufficiently butched up she) is protecting' (564)'; 'not just heroes (even when they are women)' (565). This might seem a strange illustration, yet in each instance the breaking (or blurriness) of the sex/gender boundary is clear in the sentence, a blurriness that the sentence cannot grammatically or epistemologically incorporate and so the gendered (and sexed) 'anomalies' have to be placed in parentheses/brackets.

I think this 'simple' illustration matters a great deal in regard to our thinking about the current use of the concept of military masculinities, but *less* for what it tells us about the violent workings of the military, and *more* for what it reveals about persistent commitments to binaried gender thinking – and the value of concepts. Critical scholarship tells us most clearly that work of militarized masculinities percolates through myriad sites (many non-corporeal) as well as being intertwined with a constellation of other concepts. As such, perhaps the problems we see emerging around military masculinities are less related to the apparent severing from the 'male body', and more in the kinds of answers we have expected work around it to supply – and the lingering attachment, despite critical protestations to the contrary, to gendered and sexed binary corporeality.

Does it matter whether the soldiers are men or women in the photo depicting the end of the Beslan School siege? No – at least not in that moment or in the context of the pursuance of military work. But yes, it does matter very much to how we think military violence into existence and to how we think we can suffocate its violent energies. In our intellectually disciplinary environments it seems we may still be wedded to the illusion of 'scientific methodology' via which parcels of knowledge, sense, and meaning-making can be securely manipulated into containable forms – like a concept. This is then supposed to morph into a tool, one workable and usable to move a range of agendas, hopes, and desires forward. And, as stated earlier, the concept of military masculinities is integrally connected to a wide range of feminist hopes and ambitions not limited to more obvious military sites. We can intellectually chase around the competing meanings, definitions, and work of military masculinities, as Belkin and Carver do, but I think it is important to momentarily step aside from the argumentative detail and pay closer attention to the tools we use, and to the work we hope they will do.

So – what is the problem with the concept of military masculinities? I think we have less theoretical control than the idealist, progressivist narrative of 'knowledge–concept–tool–practice' story gestured towards above implies. One only has to glance at the trails of hatred currently weaving around the globe, about many of which we, as critical scholars, imagined much of the conceptual and political work had been done to achieve their positioning as, at the very least, unacceptable. A 'concept' in the current militarized, terrorized, 'racially white' global moment seems a pretty weak thing to have so much faith in.

Notes

1. Newcastle University, November 2015.
2. Or indeed any (human) body at all including the increased use of sophisticated technologies, drones, intelligence, and cyber activity.

3. Though institutional gender discrimination would suggest the female 'military person' has to be 'better' than her male counterparts to achieve the same grade(s).
4. Currently (at time of writing) Grayson Perry (British artist) hosts a UK Channel 4 television series on 'All Man' in which he visits ultra-male worlds to explore how contemporary masculinity shapes the lives and expectations of men in Britain today. http://www.channel4.com/programmes/grayson-perry-all-man.

Disclosure statement

No potential conflict of interest was reported by the author.

References

Belkin, A. 2012. *Bring me men: Military masculinity and the Benign Facade of American Empire, 1898-2001*. Oxford: Oxford University Press.

Belkin, A., and T. Carver. 2012. Militarized masculinities and the erasure of violence. *International Feminist Journal of Politics* 14, no. 4: 558–67.

Davis, K. 2008. Intersectionality as Buzzword. A sociology of science perspective on what makes a feminist theory successful. *Feminist Theory* 9: 67–85.

Duncanson, C. 2013. *Forces for good?: Military masculinities and peacebuilding in Afghanistan and Iraq*. Basingstoke: Palgrave Macmillan.

Living archives and Cyprus: militarized masculinities and decolonial emerging world horizons

Anna M. Agathangelou

ABSTRACT

Huddled within the most influential theorisations and praxes of war and violence are imaginations of collating masculinities, texts and their embodiments. Interpreting and reading my mother as a non-dominant body, and her stories about war, violence, and Cyprus as re-iterative corporeal insights and practices challenging such toxic masculinities, I argue that such performances and embodiments (what I call living archives), albeit with multiple tensions, re-orient us to emerging decolonial horizons. In doing so, I directly challenge and unsuture the complacent IR historiographies of security and war and the ways they insist on composing and writing by bringing together certain archives (i.e., images of violent places and state documents) and silencing those which systematically and consistently point to modernity's violent frameworks including their production of violent masculinities on which extinguishment and futures lie. Such an insistence colludes with certain toxic regimes of representation expecting certain subjects, sovereigns, and institutions to order and reiterate (produce) colonial and violent racialized masculine (and racialized feminized) practices between ourselves and the world. Living archives are also those invented signs, imaginations, and excesses that press materiality and its impasses (i.e., in the form of capture, blackness, non-genders, etc. and resolution of signs and fictions), exposing the limits of modernity's fictioning, and against any resolution and labor that produces violence all the while sublating it.

Introduction

Drawing on critical postcolonial and feminist work and the living archive of my mother's voice as analytic practice, this piece challenges debates on military masculinities and war. As her narration makes clear, the creation of militaries as iconic global currencies and the concept of military masculinities used to understand these currencies are entangled with self-determination struggles. When taken seriously, these struggles demand a re-reading theory that moves us beyond gendered relations and racialized descriptive sites of militarism and war.

The Cypriot site

In its decolonization struggle against Britain, Cyprus became a geopolitical and ideological contestation site during the Cold War. As Caute explains, the superpower struggle was 'simultaneously a traditional political–military confrontation between the *pax Americana* and the *pax Sovietica* empires, ... an ideological and cultural contest on a global scale and without historical precedent' (2003, 21). North Atlantic Treaty Organization (NATO) (i.e. Turkey, Greece, Britain, the US) and the Soviet bloc vied to represent progress and human development as the embodiment of militarized masculinity in a social democratic, socialist, and non-aligned development project. Claiming a place in the world entailed alignment, with pressure to choose a side in the superpower struggle between capitalism and socialism.

> [V]iolence in the context of international relations, we realize, represents a formidable threat to the oppressed. What must be avoided at all costs are strategic risks, the espousal by the masses of an enemy doctrine and radical hatred by tens of millions of men .... Today the peaceful coexistence between the two blocs maintains and aggravates the violence in colonial countries. (Fanon 1967, 38–40)

I read Cyprus as a process and a set of social assemblages of inhabiting worlds that are constituted by the co-presence of a multiplicity of beings and relations whose worlds may assert different temporal trajectories. Structurally and logically, Cyprus expresses the conditions of politics and the possibilities of pragmatic inventions. But can Cyprus transform the violence of colonialism and the necropolitics of nationalized murders and rapes through the emergence of gendered and racialized recognitions, the creation of a sovereign state, and self-determination? Arguably, their unfolding in Cyprus problematizes a political that thrives by changing its contradictions into subsidies and extensions.

Archives and visceral grammars

To tell the story of militarized masculinities and show that the historical contestations between the West and non-West knowledge-practices (Turcotte forthcoming) constitute a shared 'veritable politics of reality', we engage the production and dominant reading theories of archives – but archives as more than tools of control. It is important to pay attention to how worlds are made by the marginalized who are concerned with those worlds and the questions raised and who have a stake in them beyond force, enslavements, and settler colonialisms. In June 2014, my mother said:

> It was one of those beautiful quiet Mays. The flowers had bloomed and their aromas filled the air. And your grandfather was telling me that story about the Venetians and the Muslims. If I remember right, it was the time when the Muslims attacked the Venetians and many of our Christians were massacred. Your grandfather used to tell me that it was in Nicosia and even the number of those civilians that were slaughtered but I can't remember now. That war led to many more deadly threats. All these fields in the village were ran by Muslims, you see the tsuvlik/χωράφι [field]? There where the stubborn shrubs protrude unexpectedly alongside dirt? That hill is drenched in the sweat of the Christians and the Muslims and even in the urine of feral dogs who were attracted to it by the smell of food.

> It was around 1959. It was probably around Easter, when Maroula's husband Panais was shot in the middle of the neighbouring village. He was a handsome man on the wrong side

of history. He was a communist. I am not sure who killed him though. Some say the right [i.e. read nationalists] and others the British. Nobody knows.

Anna: They just killed him in the middle of the village, in cold blood?

My mother: They did. He was a 'communos' [rough translation: a derogatory word for a communist] according to his killers. Others say that he was a nationalist, a member of EOKA A [the anti-colonial and nationalist movement in Cyprus]. Though some friends told me later that some from the ethnikofrones [nationalist right] always said: 'We hate doing this, we are sorry, but it's our job, after all'.

Some might argue that my mother is simply sharing her life experiences, not actively reflecting on or re-articulating meaning. But her stories engender the repetition that writes imperial wars, precisely when such stories as a structure of repetition and inquiry are denied. Possibilities live in the interstices of her stories of masculinized expressions, both imperial war contestations (Venetians, Ottomans) and nationalist (Turkish, British, Greek).

As a technology of governance, composing and writing an archive enables certain geopolitical hierarchies, empires, and abstractions by augmenting the power of some at the expense of others. But does it?

My mother: Blood, sacrifice, redemption, and salvation all become one in war. Who ends up dying, who ends up suffering? Our children. Ourselves and our communities. We co-live together for so many generations and suddenly, you are a Christian and you are a Muslim and you cannot live together. It seems that militaries are always saying slaughter is a life-giving, productive force. All for money. Those who have the bombs [nuclear power] seem to be considered the most powerful and they may end war and redeem mankind. At times, I wonder. And other times I say: Are we in the end times?

Anna: What do you mean?

My mother: Well, you know. The Bible says so in Revelations.

Anna: Mom. Those are historical texts. Those events already occurred. They are not speaking to what is to come.

Some may read this as responding generally to imperial wars. However, composing what she remembers and how she lives, a living archive this way, my mom makes a dedicated effort to address a question on the frontiers of what is knowable, despite the impossibility of knowing. The presence of her body and voice in an economy of war obscures the 'always-already-there-ness' of force and structural violence that recognize the body politic only through the lens of an imperial-nationalist yet critical militarization and masculinity and, hence, block another kind of listening, another time and world, perhaps moored to another body politic. In the storytelling, my mother may seem to conflate analytical principles (albeit with many tensions) to do a critique. However, I read her instead and the way she uses language to engage in social analysis. She seems to challenge dominant scientific criteria of knowledge production. Her words zoom in to the canonization of imperial-nation-state Eurocentric philosophies and practices that suture killing with the nation-state, while marginalizing emerging practical and poetic labours and insights, the antidotes to masculinized and imperial nationalisms that attempt to forever compromise the terrain of revolutionary possibility and justice.

My mother's analytics are a system of thought and invention, a set of theories about the interpenetration of religion, nationalisms, masculinities, and geographical material composition, and obligation to inventing how people and place could be otherwise. She composes what I call a living archive, whereby her stories act as living social sources which can narrate institutions and politics in their many tensions and otherwise. She experiments in bringing certain aspects of her world to life, political untranslatabilities as emerging configurations of wretchedness, including answering the question about whether Cyprus as an ecology and Cypriot peoples could transform the violence of imperial-nation-states and their militarized masculinities. In short, my mother's and my recomposition pushes us to re-consider, to bring a decolonial judgment into play but one without the law of a conventional thought and horizon of racist, masculinized, and militarized subjectivities. It is this testing with a language and a visceral poetics yet to be written, this moment of creation, that orients us towards a living archive whose content and or affects become expressed disarticulately. It is an advent without the jurisdictions of the sovereign and its contingent instruments of militaries and masculinities.

I asked my mother about her understanding of self-struggles, or what critics might consider the epistemologies of her stories. She challenges my questions by responding: 'That's your stuff not mine. You can figure that out if you want. I do not want to converse in that way'. She traverses visible and invisible borders, linguistically and otherwise. She attends to the multiple linguistic, relational, and affective landscapes of this very small island as frames (Mitchell 2014) as if tending to her unfinished poetry, the sacredness of life.

'Missing' Cyprus and 'missing' world

Acknowledging the theorizations and figurations of violence of our (un)making has the potential to disrupt the compulsive canonizations of our archives, living and otherwise, to generate judgement and recursivity at the seams of life. Beyond risking our own identity/human capital consumption, we risk our existence. My mother says:

> Cyprus is living, breathing, bright, noisy, loud, and above all hot. And all these people claimed that they were peacemakers bringing to us the good news telling us that the pagans were killers. Their sacrifices to the gods were backward. What have they though done to us? What is war? Isn't it a demand for us to sacrifice our kids en mass all the while raising this violence to a sacred status, raising it higher than life and death? And more than that they steal our homes and our lands. My father always used to tell us that if there is suffering in the world there is no else to look to except ourselves.[1]

If Cyprus is a crucial character, as my mother articulates, what does this character tell us about those 'missing' constitutions of the global and the political in imperial-nation-state wars underpinned by masculine militarisms? What does it tell us about the limits of the vital figuration of militarized masculinity and its power in the contemporary formation (i.e. its social reproduction) of world politics? What happens to feminist and critical security International Relations (IR) theory around its object? My mother's words remind me of the 'regret' felt by some Greek Cypriots when Papadopoulos cried in front of the whole country, mobilizing them to vote against the Annan Plan. His project orientations – mobilizing affects, meanings, disrupted revolutions, shifts in sovereign power – politically mobilized and legitimated nationalist-racialized subjects and delegimated others. Those wretched of the earth, to remember Frantz Fanon here, cannot put their wretchedness to work. Colonization and imperial-nationalist thought's governing fiction involves the resolution of figures – that is, analogies – and signs that are self-referential and cumulative and always as a refusal of the wretchedness' grammars (Fanon 1967, 212).

My own 'analytic' which itself does not reflect, represent, or explain processes but takes part in the relations, insights, and practices that compose Cyprus allows me to ask how critical narratives speaking of military might and militarization regulate historical method, from selecting and legitimating sources to organizing modes of analytics themselves, including the collation of a militarized masculine story that has a beginning and an end. Through regrets and ongoing violence, 'chosen traumas [and] certain tasks are given to the next generation' (Politics-and-Language-in-a-Changing-World.php). Consequently, accounts about Cyprus must be challenged to creatively contribute to developing/sharpening the problem of militarism and masculinity and the global landscape within which power is framed, contested, negotiated, and made possible. 'Maybe', I thought, 'My family, the community with which I align myself, is the community that subsidizes me (not only in terms of resources but in terms of ontological offering) as an adjusted "self"'. As if in response, my mother said to me:

> Do not forget (DO NOT FORGET)[2] next week, it is your uncle's funeral. They finally found his bones. Finally, your aunt is going to find some relief. What a life. For the last 34 years to be in a state of 'limbo'. Your Aunt Maria does not even want to know. She prefers waiting.
>
> Anna: But Mom, I think she knows he is dead. You already knew he was dead. Didn't your friends tell you about it? You even know where his grave is, no?

Rushing from Nicosia to Famagusta for the funeral, I had competing thoughts. Was I 'regretting' that my uncle's bones had been found? Was I disappointed with this telos? What happened to my uncle after the last time my father and I talked to him? I can only remember his face and how softly he spoke. I always go back to my father: 'Dad, what did my uncle say? Do you remember?', as if in the forgetting I shake free of the multiple historicisms. My father always makes up something. He floats the possibility of a Cyprus that does not depend on death and killing. We both keep alive that last moment, but that last event re-opens the conflict and develops it as a broader problem, some of it mediated by others, some not.

My uncle's bones were found via the Committee of the Missing in Cyprus. The United Nations (UN) and leaders Sevgul Uladag and Xenophon Kallis worked to address the 'regret' for a 'loss' that benefited nationalist and corporate agendas but not those in the community. What, then, is at stake in the search for the 'remains' of bodies 'sacrificed' during the 1974 war in Cyprus? Can UN-guided and Greek- and Turkish-led projects be totalized through a grid/matrix of governmentality? In fact, the project is not coherent and 'total', but rife with ruptures and dislocations at the heart of the sovereign and militarized projects that erected militarized masculinity as their apotheosis. In the search for the bones, we are testing our account of the hypothesized relationship among bones, earth, and the living and its co-composition of our subjectivities beyond militarisms and masculinizations, and the resulting obligations that form between Cyprus and the people. We test living-on orientations that challenge imperial and nationalist neoliberal practices, even at moments of convergence.

Thus far, the remains of 386 people have been identified. Identification has been difficult, and a lab official comments: 'Our goal is to give back a complete body, but in some cases it is impossible' (www.thenews.com.pk/daily_detail.asp?id=135659). The impossibility gestures to a question. How will '(in)complete' bodies yield answers to our questions, and which questions? If the goal is to put 'to rest' imperial-state wars and challenge the militarizations and ghosts of conflicts, this may be impossible. The excavations bring to the fore the materialities of imperial war, the new desires in the new iterations of projects like nationalism, capital formations, racializations, and the new forms of wretchedness that question them. The contestation over the seeking of the missing is broader than this humanitarian project (Agathangelou 2017).

It is time to remember the decolonial struggles, the remnants of life, located within a wretched colonial ecology, next to the geographical and historical rifts that militarized masculinities generate, haunting our future. Let's remember that the bones of our missing are integral to our compositions. Our struggles around them reveal that their dispossessed life, and incomplete death, are symptoms of the rottenness of both colonial and nationalist pathologies. Their discourses of cure are revealed to be infused with force and compulsion. Let's not forget: our visceral repetitions, and disorientations, reanimate our insurgencies for a not-yet political.

Notes

1. Special credit goes to Harry Anastasiou for our conversations on nationalism and war.
2. This slogan was mobilized by the Republic of Cyprus against the invasion and territorial conquest by Turkey of 40% of the island.

Acknowledgements

This piece is dedicated to my mother whose commitment to struggles for self-determination is unwavering. Special credit goes to Harry Anastasiou for our many conversations on nationalism and war. A special thank you also to Kyle D. Killian, Amanda Chisholm, Joanna Tidy and Elizabeth Thompson for their editing suggestions and comments.

Disclosure statement

No potential conflict of interest was reported by the author.

References

Agathangelou, A.M. 2017. Humanitarian innovations and material returns: valuation, bio-financialization, and radical politics. *Science, Technology and Society* 22, no. 1: 78–101. doi:10.1177/0971721816682803
Caute, D. 2003. *The dancer defects: The struggle for cultural supremacy during the cold war.* Oxford: Oxford University Press.
Fanon, F. 1967. *Wretched of the earth.* New York: Grove Press.
Turcotte, H. forthcoming. *Petro-sexual politics: US legal expansions, geographies of violence and the critique of justice.* University of Georgia Press.

Index